GW00362560

Carole Handslip is a trained home economist. She
has worked for Unilever, then at the Cordon Bleu
School of Cookery in London before becoming Head
of Cookery at the Cordon Bleu School at Winkfield in
Berkshire. She left to have a family and took up
part-time catering and writing, then went on to
preparing food for photography. She has written a
number of books for Sainsbury; her *Wholefood Cooking*
is the bestseller of the range. She recently
participated in BBC TV's series 'A Taste of Health'
and was involved in the preparation of the
accompanying book.

Carole Handslip

The Salad Book

Illustrated by Mike Dodd

PAN Original
Pan Books London and Sydney

First published 1986 by Pan Books Ltd
18–21 Cavaye Place, London SW10 9PG
9 8 7 6 5 4 3 2 1
© Carole Handslip 1986
Illustrations © Mike Dodd 1986
ISBN 0 330 29242 0
Photoset by Parker Typesetting Service, Leicester
Printed and bound in Great Britain by
Cox & Wyman Ltd, Reading

Contents

Dedication

To Simon, my long-suffering husband who has eaten salads
for breakfast, lunch and dinner for the last six months, for the
most part with enthusiasm!

Acknowledgements

To my children Nicholas and Susanna who have helped both
with the tasting and with preparing many of the salads.
To Bunny for her hours of work correcting errors and typing
the entire manuscript without complaint.

Introduction

Of all foods, none can provide the infinite variety of taste, texture and colour to be found in the salad bowl. Available, fresh and versatile all the year round, salads can be eaten as starter, main course, or dessert. They can be the staple diet of the vegetarian and wholefoodie or a refreshing interlude on the palate of the gourmet. A salad can be a quick, light snack for the busy dieter or an epicurean adventure for the nouvelle cuisine-nik. For the hostess, salads are a superb opportunity to display an imagination and artistry that will never be spoiled by an intemperate oven, and for the busy mother they have the great advantage that they can be prepared way in advance and produced at a moment's notice.

Salads are a health food which few need much urging to enjoy and, nowadays, with all the pressure to eat better, salads offer an easy and enjoyable alternative to some of the more faddish health-food diets. They are recognized by all leading health and nutrition experts as being beneficial. Freshly prepared salads are rich in vitamins and a valuable source of minerals and trace elements; they are also an excellent way of introducing fibre into the diet.

Above all, salads are such a very cheerful food. Whatever the season, salad ingredients are fresh and colourful; good strong flavours in winter and light crisp leaves in summer. And now that greengrocers are offering more and more exotic imports, the opportunity increases to make the salad bowl ever more interesting.

Of course the greengrocer is by no means the only source of fresh salad ingredients. Almost any green open space will furnish edible leaves for your salad bowl; even the flower garden can offer a useful supply. In November 1985 I went to Beaune with a party of friends for the 'Trois Glorieuses', the annual wine festival of Burgundy. From a weekend full of memorable meals I will always remember a glorious Salade Mesclun, prepared specially for us at the Vieux Moulin at Bouilland.

All the usual green leaves you associate with salad were tossed in a really delightful dressing based on walnut oil, together with radicchio, but what made it taste- so fresh and different was the addition of what we often think of as weeds in England. Madame had added rocket, *pissenlit* (dandelion leaves) and lamb's lettuce, and flavoured the dish with fresh herbs. In France, all these things can be bought in the markets but I was sure Madame had simply asked one of the kitchen lads to pop into the garden and pick the ingredients on the spot. Provence is the real home of Salade Mesclun, but I cannot remember a happier – or a quicker – blend of salad ingredients. (See page 84 for a recipe.)

There are a large number of very good but unusual salad ingredients. I've listed quite a number in the Glossary and they really are well worth trying. Nasturtium leaves don't sound particularly appetizing but they give a marvellous peppery taste to a salad; their flowers are stunning when set as decoration and they taste good too. Borage, marigolds, primrose, violet and chive flowers all make extremely attractive salad decoration and all are eminently edible. The list of edible leaves to be garnered from field and hedgerow is huge. I find that children, including some very old children, have enormous fun locating and gathering these plant foods for me to turn into salads. But their efforts do need supervising!

Further afield, the Middle East is an unending source of ideas for salads. Their traditional *mezze* comprise a great many small selections of different salads, many of which are real gourmet delights. Few of us would have the time to prepare a proper *mezze* of forty or more little dishes but it is certainly worth trying one or two appetizers before a meal. One of the best-known, or the most written about, is Tabbouleh (recipe page 97); a favourite of mine, it is made from bulgur wheat soaked for thirty minutes, drained thoroughly, dressed with oil and lemon and tossed with lots of parsley and mint; quite delicious. In fact I frequently prepare pre-meal nibbles based on *mezze* as a way of keeping a hungry family at bay without spoiling their appetites. Rices, beans and sprouts are easily turned into a small bowl and dressed with oil, herbs and vinegar or lemon.

Herbs play a very large part in successful salad blending, so much so that it's worth getting to know them better. There is a list of herb specialists at the back of the book and I recommend the serious 'saladier' to order a catalogue or two; you will be amazed at the number and variety available.

The increasing ease and affordability of foreign travel has given many people a new taste for exotic foods. It is extremely fortunate that the same technology that gets us there brings the new foods back. There is no doubt that tropical fruits have transformed fruit salads into sophisticated puds. For me, it's the mango that most tempts the taste buds and conjures up scenes of coral strand and limpid lagoon, but they're all quite luscious and lend themselves, with very good effect, even to savoury foods. Duck à l'Orange is well known, but have you tried Tropical Prawns, a delightful concoction of papaya, avocado and prawn (page 58)? Equally different, but nearer home, is Strawberry and Cucumber Salad (page 00), a fresh and most attractive starter to any meal.

I attach a great deal of importance to getting the balance of a meal just right. Taste, texture and colour are all essential to proper enjoyment of what you are eating. I would seldom serve a leafy salad vinaigrette with a main course but nearly always after, so that people are better able to appreciate the sharp fresh taste in contrast with the richer flavours of the main dish. I've carried this idea into the book by arranging the chapters into starters, side salads, snacks, main meals, etcetera; not only will this arrangement narrow your field of search for an appropriate salad but might, I hope, encourage you to experiment with some of the more unusual salads on offer. Kohlrabi Vinaigrette (page 117), Gado Gado (page 146), Bazargan (page 98), Scandinavian Herring Salad (page 132), Okra Salad (page 118) and Caponata (page 68) are all very pleasant, if different, variations on the salad theme.

But they all depend on being well dressed. With the possible exception of mayonnaise, most dressings are quick and easy to prepare; little cooking skill is needed, just a good eye and a strong wrist. It is important to use the best ingredients. Corn oil, worthy as it may be in the kitchen, will never achieve the wonderful, evocative taste of pure, green, cold pressed olives. Vinegar too is worth investigating. Discard your malt variety in favour of a wine or fruit vinegar – the taste is infinitely superior and will repay the extra cost in extra pleasure. I particularly enjoy raspberry vinegar.

In short, whether eaten on their own as a snack or main meal, or as an accompaniment to other food, salads are a really worthwhile food in their own right, well worth the trouble of careful selection and preparation and immediately capable of demonstrating the art and ingenuity of the preparer. I think salads are fun.

OILS, VINEGARS AND SEASONINGS

The principal ingredients in a salad dressing are oil and vinegar, with a variety of other flavourings that can be varied to suit the particular ingredients in the salad.

It is most important to use the best ingredients, and the choice of oil is especially important.

OILS

Oils are produced from various nuts, seeds and beans and each has its own particular flavour. Unrefined oils have a superior flavour, and although more expensive than refined oils, they are worth using for salad dressings.

Olive oil

This is the best oil for most salad dressings as its flavour is far superior to others. Choose a green-tinged, fruity oil which will be labelled 'extra virgin' or 'first pressing', as the flavour will be richer.

Sesame oil

This has a strong, nutty tang which gives an unusual flavour to dressings and is particularly good with oriental-type salads.

Sunflower and Safflower oil

These are neutral-flavoured oils and can be mixed with olive oil, or used alone, to produce a lighter dressing. They both have the advantage of being high in polyunsaturates.

Mayonnaise made with a combination of one of these oils and olive oil has a lighter consistency.

Walnut oil

Walnut oil has the most wonderful flavour and aroma, and is usually mixed with olive oil in a French dressing. It is especially good with slightly bitter salad plants such as chicory, radicchio, dandelions or spinach.

VINEGARS

Good-quality wine, cider or herb-flavoured vinegars are essential for a good dressing – malt vinegar is far too harsh. Lemon juice can be used instead if you prefer.

Brown rice vinegar is used largely in Japanese cooking, so is suitable for oriental-based salads.

Cider vinegar is reputed to have many healthy properties and valuable nutrients. It also has a light, subtle flavour.

Wine vinegar is the one most commonly used for French dressing; either red or white will do.

Flavoured vinegars can be made from any of the above varieties. To do this, steep your chosen flavouring in a small bottle of vinegar for anything up to three weeks. Particularly good additions are basil, tarragon, garlic, chive flowers, thyme, mint and rosemary. Raspberry wine vinegar can be made by adding about twelve raspberries to a bottle of vinegar. Strain them into clean bottles and store until required.

Bottles of home-made herb vinegars also make excellent gifts.

MUSTARDS

Mustards vary considerably in strength and flavour. The ones I use most frequently are:

Dijon mustard

This is made from husked and ground mustard seeds, white wine vinegar and spices. It has a smooth texture and is the most versatile for salads. It is made in Dijon in France, and only mustard made there may be labelled as such.

German mustard

Flavoured with herbs and spices, this mustard is quite mild and has a sweet-sour taste. I use it in Scandinavian and German salads.

Moutarde de Meaux

This is made with partly ground whole mustard seeds, so has a grainy texture and is aromatic. A delicious flavour, but sometimes you may not want to see the grains on the salad.

SEASONINGS

Black peppercorns

These are sun-dried green peppercorns of the pepper vine, and have far more flavour if they are freshly ground from the mill.

Salt

Sea salt is the variety I use, because it is less refined. It is available in both fine and crystal form.

GARNISHES

Garnishes can be purely decorative or can add an essential culinary quality to a salad.

Flowers

The most colourful of all garnishes. Use individual petals or the whole flower, depending on the size and type, and sprinkle over the salad after tossing and just before serving.

Herbs

A variety of freshly picked green herbs makes one of the best salad garnishes. Sometimes chop and sprinkle them, sometimes use whole sprigs, such as mint or lemon balm. Feathery fronds of fennel are exquisite laid over a creamy dressing.

Nuts and Seeds

These make a very attractive garnish on a variety of salads. All are improved by browning first, as this brings out the nutty flavour (see page 35).

Spices

Paprika, cayenne or chilli pepper can be sprinkled on salads coated with a creamy yoghurt or smetana dressing.

Cucumber cones and curls

Slice the cucumber thinly, then make a cut along the radius of each slice. Hold each side and twist round to form a cone. To make a curl, hold the slice vertically and twist one end to the right and one to the left.

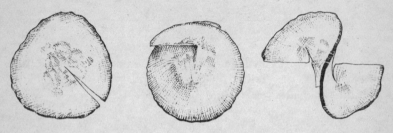

Lemon cones and curls can be made in the same way.

Radish chrysanthemums

Remove the stalk, and with a sharp knife cut downwards across the radish at 2-mm ($\frac{1}{10}$-inch) intervals, keeping the radish joined at the base. Then cut in the opposite direction to form minute squares. Drop into iced water for about an hour, until it opens out.

Radish roses

Remove the stalk, and with the pointed end of a vegetable knife cut petal shapes round the bottom half of the radish, keeping them joined at the base. Cut a second row of petals in between and above the first row, and so on until you reach the top of the radish. Drop into iced water for about an hour until it opens out.

Radish waterlily

Remove the stalk, and using a small vegetable knife cut downwards 6 to 8 times, making a cross and keeping the radish joined at the base. Drop into iced water for about an hour until it opens out.

Spring onion tassels

Trim a spring onion to about 7.5cm (3 inches) long. Cut lengthways through the green part of the onion several times, to within 4cm (1½ inches) of the end. Place in a bowl of iced water for about an hour to allow the ends to curl up.

Tomato flowers

Use a firm tomato and with a sharp knife pare off the skin in a continuous strip about 1cm (½ inch) wide, starting at the smooth end. With the flesh side inward start to curl from the base end, forming a bud shape. Continue winding the strip of skin into a flower.

HERBS AND FLOWERS

HERBS

Herbs, which used to be so integral a part of English cookery, are being rediscovered. Their use in any form of cooking is much to be recommended, but in salads the addition of their fresh, aromatic leaves is of special value.

Do not be afraid to experiment. There are so many herbs from which to choose, such a variety of flavours and aromas and even colours, that you can ring the changes constantly.

Herbs are now becoming generally available in supermarkets, but there is a special fascination in growing your own in the kitchen garden, or even in window boxes. For those of you interested in growing your own herbs, there is a list of suppliers on page 188, all of whom can supply by mail.

Basil

A wonderful, pungent herb with large, soft light green leaves. It is especially good with tomatoes, and is the key ingredient in the well-known Italian sauce *pesto*.

Chervil

This parsley-like plant has delicate, feathery leaves and is one of the *fines herbes* used in French cuisine. It has a light, subtle flavour which blends well with other herbs, and is an attractive garnish.

Chives

Useful for both their leaves and flowers, chives are the mildest of the onion family and should always be used raw, which makes them ideal for salads. They give a good contrast in colour and flavour to pale, creamy dressings, and combine well with other herbs in a vinaigrette.

Always cut them with a sharp knife or scissors to avoid bruising. The flowers, which bloom in early summer, have a strong flavour. Each floret should be pulled gently from the round flower head and sprinkled on salads for garnish.

Coriander

Sometimes called Cilantro, or Chinese parsley, it looks similar to flat-leaved parsley, but you can soon tell the difference by rubbing the leaves; coriander has a distinctive, pungent smell. It is obtainable in Greek, Chinese and Indian shops, and increasingly in supermarkets. It is used extensively in India, Asia, the Middle East, Mexico and South America in its fresh, leafy form. The seeds are used as an ingredient in curry powder; they can also be ground to a powder and used to good effect in many cooked vegetable salads.

Dill

Dill, or Dillweed as it is sometimes called, blends well with fish. It is also used to flavour pickled cucumbers, and enhances cucumber and potato salads. Dill is widely used in Scandinavia, Central Europe and Russia. It has a slightly sharp yet sweet flavour.

Fennel

In appearance fennel closely resembles dill, but has a sweet, aniseed flavour which is quite different. Like dill, it has long been used as a herb in fish dishes and is also good with beetroot and cucumber salads. The extremely pretty, feathery leaves make an excellent garnish.

Horseradish

The grated root has a hot, biting taste and is most often used raw. When not available fresh, it can be bought ready in jars or as a ready-prepared relish. It is an excellent flavouring to use with smoked fish or beef salads.

Lemon balm

Lemon balm, or sweet balm, is a fragrant lemon-scented plant with a delicate flavour. It is excellent in both fruit and vegetable salads and the smaller leaves make a pretty garnish for fruit salads.

Marjoram

There are several varieties of marjoram, sweet marjoram being the best variety for cooking; it is sweet and spicy, but quite mild. Wild marjoram, or oregano, has the strongest flavour and is best dried, when it is used in Provençal dishes and pizza. Chopped with other herbs it is a good addition to a vinaigrette dressing and is also good with peppers, tomatoes and aubergines.

Mint

There are many varieties of mint, but from the cook's point of view spearmint and Bowles' mint are the two most useful.

Spearmint is the common, or garden, mint, best known in Britain, with smooth, dark green leaves. Bowles' mint is the largest of all the mints and has soft downy leaves with a superior flavour. It is excellent used in vinaigrette dressings and also blends well with yogurt. Delicious with mangetouts and with fruit-based salads, such as melon vinaigrette.

Nasturtium

Nasturtium is a round-leaved trailing or climbing plant, and is useful in the herb garden as the leaves, flowers and seeds can all be used in cooking. The leaves have a hot, peppery flavour and are an excellent addition to blander salads.

Parsley

The most familiar varieties are the curly-leaved and flat-leaved, or French parsley. Hamburg parsley is another flat-leaved variety, grown also for its roots, which may be used as a winter vegetable.

They are all rich in vitamin C and valuable in the daily diet. Parsley has so many uses – as part of a bouquet garni, in a mixture of *fines herbes*, as a garnish and as a salad ingredient. It is also useful in dishes which contain garlic, as it softens the flavour.

Chewing a sprig of parsley is reputed to clear the breath after eating garlic or onion.

Purslane

Purslane has fleshy stalks and rosettes of succulent green leaves which have a sharp, clean flavour. It is an excellent addition to green salads and is widely used in France, the Middle East and Arab countries.

Rocket (*Roquette* in French, *Rugola* in Italian)

The young green leaves of this plant have a distinctive, warm, peppery flavour and are delicious in green salads. A particularly good ingredient for the Provençal Salade Mesclun, it is not often seen in Britain, although it is easy to cultivate.

Savory

Winter and summer savory are very similar, but the former has a coarser flavour. They are both fairly strong, aromatic herbs, with long, narrow leaves. Savory is best used as a cooking herb and is included here because of its affinity with beans.

Tarragon

A very aromatic and distinctive herb. There are two varieties, French and Russian, the former being far superior in flavour.

Tarragon is part of the classic *fines herbes* mixture, and gives an excellent flavour to green and raw vegetable salads. Tarragon vinegar can be made by steeping the fresh herb in white wine vinegar, and used to make summery vinaigrettes.

Thyme

This is one of the most useful and best-known herbs, garden thyme and lemon thyme being the most popular varieties.

The fragrant leaves of garden thyme are an essential ingredient in a bouquet garni. Thyme has a fairly strong flavour, but a little chopped thyme of either variety is an excellent addition to a vinaigrette dressing.

FLOWERS

The fascination of flowers or flower petals as an attractive garnish for salads was discovered by our ancestors long ago. Apart from the delightful flavour of many, the colour contrasts they provide are their main asset.

Common sense will be the best guide to which flowers may be used whole and which should have the petals gently separated from the centre pad, or calyx.

It is, of course, important that the flowers should look fresh and clean, so should they need to be washed, handle with great care and pat dry with soft kitchen paper. They can then be stored in a sealed polythene bag in the refrigerator until required.

Sprinkle them over the top of the salad just before serving, so that they do not become marked by the dressing.

Borage

The brilliant blue flowers of this herb have a sweet flavour and look wonderful in salads. They have hairy sepals behind the petals, which should be removed just before using.

Chives

Chives have pretty, round mauve flower heads and a strong flavour. Pull each separate floret from the head and sprinkle over salads such as potato vinaigrette, just before serving.

Nasturtium

The flowers have long spurs and come in all shades from pale yellow and orange to pink and red. They have a piquancy that adds good flavour as well as brilliant colour to a salad.

Pot marigold

These bright colourful double or single flowers come in all shades of orange and yellow, from early spring until the frosts arrive.

Gently pull the petals from the flower head and sprinkle on the salad just before serving. They have a sweet, fairly strong flavour.

Primrose

Very little flavour, but a very pretty addition to salads in spring.

Rose petals

Wild or cultivated roses can be used in salads, but choose those with most fragrance, as they impart a delicate flavour.

GLOSSARY OF INGREDIENTS

Apples

Choose native apples whenever possible; they are full of flavour. My favourites are Russets, Cox's Orange Pippins and Worcester Pearmains, but there are many other very good varieties which deserve to be more widely used. Generally I do not peel them, as the skin adds colour and fibre to the salad. When sliced they should be tossed in the dressing immediately to prevent them turning brown.

Arame – see Sea vegetables.

Artichoke – globe

This is the flower head of a type of thistle, in season from June to October. They can be served cold with a vinaigrette or warm with hollandaise sauce. Artichoke hearts are sold canned and are useful in a variety of salads.

Artichoke – Jerusalem

A very useful winter vegetable, available from October onwards; it has a strong yet subtle flavour. The name is thought to be a corruption of the word *girasole*, the Italian name for the sunflower plant, to which it is related. I rarely peel them, as the skin provides flavour and fibre.

Asparagus

The asparagus season runs from spring to early summer. There are two basic types, green and white. A thinner version of the green variety is known as 'sprue'. Generally, the thicker the shoots, the more expensive they are. The thicker varieties usually need the coarse outer skin to be peeled off before cooking, to make them more tender.

Aubergine, or Eggplant

This large satin-skinned vegetable is available in many different shapes and the colour ranges from deep purple to white; it is available all the year round. The flesh is always eaten cooked and is used in many Mediterranean and Middle Eastern dishes. Before cooking, *dégorger* the aubergines to remove their bitter and indigestible juices. To do this, place the sliced or diced vegetable in a colander, sprinkle with salt and leave for about 30 minutes. Rinse well and dry with kitchen paper to remove excessive salt. This also reduces the amount of oil absorbed when frying.

Avocado pear

Avocados are available between late autumn and early spring, and come in many different varieties.

The Ettinger avocado is medium to large with thin, smooth, mid-green skin.

The Fuerte is smaller than the Ettinger and characteristically pear-shaped, with a speckled green skin and greenish flesh.

The Nabal is almost spherical in shape, with a dark green skin tinged with crimson.

The Hass is the smallest, and is easily recognizable by its purple, knobbly skin.

Avocados should be eaten when the skin is quite soft. To test for ripeness, cradle the fruit in the palm of your hand – it should yield to gentle pressure. To hasten ripening, keep in a bowl with other fruits. Once cut, avocados should be brushed with lemon juice to avoid discoloration. To halve an avocado cut round the centre vertically, using a sharp knife, twist the fruit and lift off the free half. To remove the stone, chop at it with a large sharp knife and it will become embedded. Give a sharp twist and it will come away on the knife.

Batavia – see Lettuce.

Beans

Broad beans are in season from May to October. Their thick furry-lined pods are usually discarded and the succulent green kidney-shaped beans are blanched, making a good basis for many salads. If picked young and small, they are delicious cooked and eaten, pod and all, in a vinaigrette dressing.

French beans are in season in Britain from June to October, but as they are now cultivated throughout the world they are available nearly all the year round. Choose beans that are of similar size and maturity, so that they cook evenly.

Dried beans – see Dried beans and pulses.

Bean sprouts

These are available throughout the year and, although you can buy them in most supermarkets, they can be grown at home with very little trouble. The seeds need no soil, no cultivating or weeding, and do not even need sunlight. All you have to do is water them.

Although you do not need special equipment to produce them, it makes the process easier if you use a special seed sprouter.

Sprouts are nutritionally an excellent food; they contain valuable amounts of vitamin C and the B complex group. They also contain a high level of protein and amino acids.

Some sprouts are good sources of vitamins E, G, K and U. Legumes generally have a higher vitamin C content, but grains contain more vitamin B.

Sprouts are fun to grow and are especially useful in winter, when salad ingredients are less varied and more expensive.

1. Pick over the seeds carefully, removing any stems and stones.
2. Put 2 tablespoons of seeds in a jar and soak overnight to encourage them to germinate more quickly.
3. Drain off the water in a sieve then cover with a damp cloth to help keep the moisture content at the right level, or put into a seed sprouter.

4. Put them out of direct sunlight. They need good ventilation and a constant temperature.
5. Run them under cold water twice a day; if the sprouts are not properly drained they can go mouldy. Be careful not to treat them roughly, or you may damage the delicate shoots.

The sprouts will increase in volume by 4 to 6 times within 2 to 6 days, depending on the pulse or grain. Once the sprouts have grown to the same length as the pulse or grain, they are ready to use. Rinse them once more and store them in the refrigerator in a covered container. They will stay fresh for up to 3 days.

The easiest to sprout are mustard and cress, mung and aduki beans, alfalfa and whole lentils. Split beans or seeds and cracked wheat will not sprout.

Beetroot

Although available most of the year, this is best in early summer when small and tender. Beetroot is delicious grated and served raw, but is more usually cooked and eaten cold in salads.

Broccoli

Broccoli is related to the cauliflower; there are several varieties.

Purple sprouting is available from winter to early spring and has a distinct purple head with dark green leaves.

Purple hearting resembles a cauliflower in size.

Calabrese, or green broccoli, is imported most of the year from Israel and Spain. It has green, fleshy stalks and compact green florets.

Brussels sprouts

These grow from tall, woody stems and are best eaten when very small, and cooked just long enough to retain some firmness. They are a winter vegetable, available from autumn to spring.

Cabbage

Spring cabbages are smooth-leaved, loose and have small hearts.

Spring greens are young cabbages with no hearts.

Savoy cabbages have dark, crinkly leaves and are in season from late autumn to early spring.

All these varieties are excellent used in salads, but cut away the central core and coarse ribs and shred them very finely, or you may find them too chewy.

Dutch cabbage, or winter whites, are used for coleslaw.

Red cabbage is used more extensively in Europe, and especially in Scandinavia. It makes a good salad if sliced thinly, and is also delicious cooked with onion and apple.

Chinese cabbage – see Lettuce.

Cauliflower

Cauliflower is in season during the early summer and in autumn. Outside these seasons, although often available, it can be very expensive. It makes an excellent salad, both raw and blanched – but blanch for only 2 minutes, as it should remain *al dente*!

Celeriac

Celeriac is in season from early autumn until February. It is a root vegetable which looks somewhat like a small swede with a wrinkled skin. It has a fine flavour similar to that of celery, and is well worth using in salads.

Celeriac can be grated raw, or cut into julienne strips and blanched for 2 minutes. To avoid discoloration, celeriac should be dressed immediately.

Celery

Home-grown blanched autumn and winter celery has the best flavour, and is available from September to April. There is also a home-grown green summer variety, but green celery is imported throughout the year from Israel, Belgium and Spain. The leaves of celery, though sometimes a little bitter eaten raw, are excellent chopped in soups and stews.

Chicory

The French and Americans call this endive, but what we know as endive, they call chicory.

Chicory is available from autumn to spring and, with its slightly bitter flavour, makes an interesting and tasty addition to winter salads. The cream and green *chicons*, literally the teeth of chicory, keep very well wrapped in a polythene bag and stored in the refrigerator.

Courgettes

Courgettes imported from Kenya and the Mediterranean are available for most of the year, but I prefer to use the home-grown variety which are cheap and plentiful in the summer months. In salads courgettes can be served raw, thinly sliced, but I prefer to marinate them in a French dressing for a few hours to soften them. Yellow courgettes are also available, and look very pretty in salads.

Cucumbers

There are two varieties, the hothouse cucumber, which is long and thin with a smooth skin; and the stubby, rough-skinned variety known as the ridge cucumber. The hothouse cucumber is available all the year round, but both are at their best during the summer months. I do not usually peel the hothouse variety, but ridge cucumbers do have tougher skins which may prove indigestible, so I prefer to peel them.

Dandelion leaves

These should be picked in early spring, as the leaves become bitter after the flowers bloom. They may be blanched by placing a bucket over the growing plant for several days; this will render them less bitter. Used in small quantities they make an excellent addition to a green salad.

Dried beans and pulses

All beans and pulses make delicious salads, but all except lentils need to be soaked overnight.

One common objection to pulses is that they cause flatulence, but this can be avoided by taking care in the preparation and initial cooking. Drain off all the water in which they have been soaking, cover with fresh water and boil for 10 minutes, then drain again. This process will destroy any harmful toxins that may be present and remove most of the substances that give rise to flatulence.

Always add salt towards the end of cooking time, as it toughens the skins and lengthens the cooking time if added sooner. If you add a strip of kombu, a type of seaweed, to the cooking water, this helps to soften pulses and improves the flavour.

Always add the dressing to cooked beans and pulses while they are still warm, as they absorb the flavour more fully. For convenience and to save fuel I tend to cook large quantities of beans when I have the time, pack them in 125g (4oz) or 250g (8oz) quantities and freeze for future use. They can then be defrosted and ready to use in about 2 hours.

Endive

A slightly bitter-tasting but most attractive curly-leaved salad plant, available from September to April. There are two varieties, the *Curly endive*, which has a mophead of light green frilly leaves, and the *Batavian endive*, also called escarole, which has broader, smoother leaves.

Before they mature, both varieties have their leaves tied together to blanch the centres, which produce light-coloured, tender inner leaves.

Avoid endives that look limp, withered or at all slimy, as they will have lost a lot of their flavour. When packed fresh in a polythene bag they keep well in the refrigerator.

Fennel

Imported bulb or Florence fennel is available throughout the year, but home-grown fennel is in season in late summer and early autumn.

Remove and discard any tough, blemished outer stalks, cut in half lengthways and slice very thinly. The flavour is fresh and crisp in texture, highly aromatic, slightly sweet, with a taste of aniseed.

Figs

Fresh figs have a fragrant perfume and are very sweet. They have green, purple or black skins, and are cultivated extensively in the Mediterranean. All varieties contain a fabulous deep red pulp interior. They can be peeled, but this is not necessary.

Garlic

Garlic is available throughout the year. The best – in my opinion – is from France, but wherever it comes from choose garlic which is firm and has no sign of mould. Garlic is a strong antiseptic, and is renowned for its health-giving properties.

I find it useful to make a garlic purée by crushing several cloves with a little salt. Place it in a screw-top jar and fill up with oil. Then either use the garlic-flavoured oil or, if you need a stronger flavour, scoop out a little of the purée from the bottom of the jar.

Grains

Grains and cereals are probably the most important staple food in the world, and most of them make excellent salads. I nearly always use them unrefined as they have a far more interesting flavour, and provide valuable fibre in the diet as well as many nutrients.

As with pulses, always pour the dressing over while the grain is warm, as more flavour will be absorbed.

Guava

Guavas have the most exotic, fragrant perfume of any fruit, and the scent fills the air of any fruiterer's when they are in stock. They have an unusual texture, slightly gritty and pulpy, and contain small seeds. Although they smell wonderful at any time, their smell is not an indication of ripeness. Wait until the skin is yellow and the flesh is soft. To be truthful, tinned guavas are one of the few fruits that I find more exotic than the original – they give a tropical touch to fruit salads.

Kiwi fruit

This is native to China, but is now grown in many countries, principally New Zealand. When ripe it has a perfumed flavour. The skin is hairy and should be removed to reveal the beautiful brilliant green flesh. Slice thinly and use in both fruit and savoury salads.

Kohlrabi

This is an interesting vegetable which has cabbage-like leaves and a large swollen stem. The stem, which is the part you eat, may be purple or green according to variety and has a flavour similar to turnip.

Leeks

Leeks are in season during the autumn and winter, but in summer the immature finger-thick plants, cooked for about 4 minutes and served with a vinaigrette dressing, make a super salad.

Winter leeks are often too harsh when used raw, and are better marinated for a few hours in a dressing which will soften them and mellow their pungent flavour.

Lettuce

Round, or cabbage, lettuce is the one most familiar to us all. I try to avoid the hothouse variety as the leaves are extremely limp and floppy.

Cos, or Romaine lettuce is a superb, crisp lettuce used especially in Caesar salad. It has long, narrow, bright green leaves, and is in season from October to February.

Iceberg lettuce has pale green, densely packed leaves which are curly at the ends. Iceberg may appear expensive when compared by size, but is extremely good value when compared by weight. It has a fresh, crisp texture and will keep well, cling film-wrapped, in the refrigerator.

Lamb's lettuce is so called because its dark green leaves resemble a lamb's tongue. It is also known as corn salad and the French call it *mâche*. It is easy to grow in the garden, and will withstand the frost. Well worth looking out for when it is in season during the autumn and winter months.

Chinese leaves are a most useful salad ingredient, available during the autumn and winter months. I like to shred it fairly finely and use it as a base, adding beanshoots and leaves such as watercress and/or dandelion.

Mangetout peas

These are also called snow peas and sugar peas. They are grown for their tender pods, and should be bought only when small, so that the tiny peas barely show their shape through the pod. They should be topped and tailed, pulling the stalk backwards towards the tip, to remove the string along the side. They are excellent in salads, and the already delicious flavour can be improved by the addition of a little mint.

Mango

This fruit is native to India, and has a truly exotic aroma. The skin may be yellow, green or pink-red, but the fruit is always yellow – and glorious. It has a unique flavour reminiscent of a mixture of peaches, nectarines and pineapples.

Melon

Melon is a very versatile fruit with firm, sweet flesh, excellent for use in a variety of salads both sweet and savoury. The skin of a ripe melon should be slightly soft at the stalk end, and some varieties will have a fragrant smell even before being cut. The shells of the smaller varieties can be reserved for use as attractive individual salad bowls. Melon seeds are edible; washed, dried and oven-toasted, they can be served as nibbles with drinks.

If storing cut melon, wrap well in clingfilm before placing in the refrigerator, or the flavour will permeate everything else.

Cantaloupe is easily recognized by its unusual skin which has a network of raised whitish veins in an intricate all-over pattern. The flesh is yellow, sweet and very fragrant.

Charentais has a pale yellow skin divided by a series of greenish lines into pronounced sections, somewhat reminiscent of Elizabethan hose. The flesh is orange and extremely sweet.

Galia has a skin very similar in appearance to the Cantaloupe, but is much more yellow when ripe. The flesh is green and sweet.

Honeydew is perhaps the best-known melon. It has a brightish yellow skin and is distinctly oval in shape. The flesh is pale green and has a more delicate flavour than other varieties. At its best it is superb, but it can be rather tasteless and in need of help. Prosciutto, port or, in extreme cases, powdered ginger will all enhance the honeydew.

Ogen, a small cannonball, is similar in shape to the Charentais but has a yellow skin, mottled green. The yellow-green flesh is sweet and succulent.

Watermelons are usually very dark green, and mostly water. The flesh is a most attractive bright red, and at its best is sweet and very refreshing. The unique colour and texture make water-melon an attractive and palatable addition to both sweet and savoury salads.

Mushrooms

Mushrooms come in so many shapes and sizes that they deserve a book to themselves, and I do recommend experimenting with the edible varieties of this vastly underrated fungus. In most of the recipes I have used button mushrooms, as their shape is so pretty. However, to make up for their comparative lack of flavour I always marinate them, sliced, in a herb vinaigrette for 30 minutes or so before tossing with the other ingredients.

Nuts

Nuts are all wonderful additions to salads, contributing a pleasant crunchiness as well as flavour. Many nuts are enhanced by browning before use; these include almonds, hazelnuts, pine nuts and peanuts.

Okra

Also known as ladies' fingers or gumbo, *bindi* in India and *bamia* in the Middle East. Delicious cooked with tomatoes and garlic, and served cold as a salad.

Onions

Onions vary enormously in their strength, so you may need to exercise a certain amount of discretion in the quantity you use. The milder Spanish onions are perhaps better in salads.

I think that spring onions, or scallions, are the best of all for salads and I like to slice them diagonally, very thinly, to give attractive, long, oval shapes. Don't use just the white bulb; the green stems are equally good to eat.

Palm hearts

Palm hearts are the tender terminal shoots of certain palm trees. They are sold pre-cooked and canned, and make an excellent addition to many salads.

Papaya

Also known as paw paw, this fruit has yellowish freckled skin and pink flesh. The subtle flavour is somewhat similar to melon with a hint of apricot, but has a much smoother texture.

Papayas are to be found throughout Africa and the Caribbean, where they have long been recognized as being much more than a delicious fruit. The plant is known locally as the Medicine Tree, and indeed the fruit has been proved to have unique healing and other medicinal qualities. It is an excellent source of vitamins A and C, calcium, iron, phosphorus and niacin.

Parsnips

Parnsips are not often used in salads, which is a pity as their sweet, unusual flavour creates an interesting change. When grated and tossed in a French dressing they make a delicious winter salad.

Pears

There are many varieties of pear, but my favourite is the William. It has a strong, pleasant scent and, when ripe, has a good strong flavour. Conference and Comice pears, firmer and not quite so sweet, are also good varieties to use, both in savoury and sweet salads.

Once ripe, pears deteriorate very quickly, so keep a wary eye on them.

Peppers

Sweet peppers, or capsicums, come in many colours and sizes. Green, yellow and red are the most common, the yellow and red being sweeter and more expensive.

When using peppers in salads remove only the seeds and any excess pith, not the skins.

Potatoes

There are almost as many varieties of potato as there are apples and, like apples, they all have different textures and flavours. Not all greengrocers label their potatoes, but where possible it is always best to choose a waxy variety for salads; these include Désirée, Maris Piper and Kipfler, and all new potatoes. New potatoes are ideal for salads, especially the small ones, which can simply be scrubbed and left in their skins. In fact no new potato should be peeled, as the skin provides a great deal of taste and goodness.

Don't forget the herbs. I always add a few to enliven the taste. Chopped dill, cucumber, shredded sorrel or nasturtium leaves should also do the trick. Always dress potato salads while they are still warm, so that the flavour of the dressing will penetrate them.

Pulses – see Dried beans and pulses.

Radicchio

This is a variety of chicory, originating in Italy. It looks rather like a small, tightly packed red lettuce, and is available from autumn to spring. It is quite expensive but comparatively few leaves are needed, as it has quite a bitter flavour. The leaves are a deep purple with a white contrasting rib, and add character to any green salad.

Radish

There are many varieties of summer radishes available. The roots may be round, oval or spindle-shaped, and vary in colour from red to pink and white, but they all have the same peppery taste. They are all very useful in salads, or to serve whole as an hors d'oeuvre.

Daikon, or Japanese white radish, is also useful for salads. It is milder than our red radish, and is pleasant grated and tossed in a dressing, or pickled.

Rice – see Grains.

Sea vegetables

Seaweeds are among the oldest foods known to man. There are many varieties, all of which are very high in vitamins and minerals. Arame is one I particularly like in salads; it has a mild sweet flavour and is rich in iodine and calcium. Hiziki can be used in a similar way. Kombu is useful when cooking beans of any type, as it helps to soften them. Nori, or Dulse, is used in the preparation of Sushi (page 48) and is also delicious toasted over a naked flame or grilled, crumbled and sprinkled over salads. All these can be bought in wholefood or Japanese food shops.

Seeds

There are many seeds that add interest and flavour to salads. My favourites are sesame, pumpkin and sunflower seeds. I often sprinkle them over salads to add flavour and interest. They taste even better if browned first, and this is done by shaking them over heat for about three minutes in a heavy-based pan. When they begin to pop, put the lid on the pan to stop them jumping out.

Sesame paste

Sesame paste, or tahini, is made from ground sesame seeds. The darker variety is the one I use, because the seed husk has been retained and this provides essential fibre. Widely used in the Middle East as a flavouring, it is also delicious in salad dressings.

Shoyu

Shoyu is naturally fermented soy sauce, made from soya beans with wheat or barley, as distinct from the commercially available varieties which frequently omit the fermentation process and contain sugar and other additives. Shoyu makes an excellent flavouring for dressings, but it is quite salty, so be careful not to overseason.

Smetana

Smetana is a cross between soured cream and yogurt and comes in two varieties. Creamed smetana contains 10% fat, whereas regular smetana contains only 5% fat. Very useful to give a creamy taste to dressings, and also to serve with fruit salads.

Sorrel

Sorrel can be picked wild from the fields, but this is sharper than the French sorrel which can easily be grown in the garden. It has an astringent, lemony flavour which is delicious in salads if used in small quantities, as a herb rather than as a vegetable.

Spinach

Uncooked spinach leaves are delicious, but as they can be a little bitter, use the young, newly sprouted leaves. Lightly blanched and chopped spinach also makes a very tasty salad, especially with yogurt dressing.

Sprouts – see Bean sprouts.

Sweetcorn

Sweetcorn is in season in late summer and is excellent in salads. Boil the cobs for about eight minutes and cool, hold them vertically on a chopping board, and slice off the kernels with a sharp knife.

Both frozen and tinned sweetcorn are suitable to use out of season, and are particularly good with finely shredded raw spring greens in shoyu dressing.

Tahini – see Sesame paste.

Tofu

Tofu is a soya bean curd made from a ground soya bean and water mixture which is boiled, strained and pressed to form cakes. It is very high in protein and lends itself to a variety of uses. It is available from Chinese supermarkets and natural food stores as silken tofu, which is a lightly pressed soya bean curd and is ideal blended in dressings. There is also a very firm tofu made by exerting heavy pressure on the bean curd to squeeze out the water content. This firm tofu is ideal to dice and marinate for use in salads. Regular tofu has a texture between these two extremes.

Tomatoes

Tomatoes are the one crop I always have time to grow for myself in the greenhouse; they are so vastly superior to the majority of those you can buy. I like to grow the large Alicante or Marmande varieties, which are juicy and full of flavour. They are available in shops throughout the year, but the flavour deteriorates after the hot summer months. At the other extreme, tiny cherry tomatoes make an interesting and delicious addition to salads. Not only do they taste sweet, they look sweet too.

Water chestnut

This has no relationship to the sweet chestnut grown in Europe. It is a tuber, cultivated in China and Japan, and used sliced in salads.
Outside Asia it is available only in tins.

Watercress

Watercress has a fresh, peppery taste that recommends it to many salads. It is available throughout the year but is not so good in summer when flowering, or during spring when the leaves are very small.

Yogurt

Yogurt is a very popular fermented milk product which is easily digested. Used in salad dressings, it is an extremely useful alternative to oil. It can also be mixed with whipped cream to give a less fatty, but equally delicious, topping to fruit salads.

Ingredients in the recipes that may be unfamiliar have been marked with an asterisk. This indicates that an explanation of what that ingredient is, and where you can get it, appears in the Glossary.

Preparation of Salad Vegetables

Preparation of vegetables for salads should be undertaken with care, especially remembering that most salad greens bruise very easily.

Wash them in cold salted water which will remove any insects or slugs from the leaves. Dry them thoroughly either in a salad spinner or shaker or by swinging them in a clean tea towel in the garden. Any water left on the leaves will dilute the dressing.

If the salad is not required immediately it can be stored in a polythene bag in the chilling compartment of the refrigerator.

Do not cut leaves; even a sharp knife will bruise the leaves and cause them to wilt more quickly. Similarly if a dressing is applied too early, the acid will cause wilting. Ideally salad greens should be torn into manageable pieces and tossed at the last moment before eating, in a large bowl. The tossed salad can then be transferred into a clean salad bowl for presentation to the table.

While some vegetables used in salads will obviously require peeling and stringing, it is undoubtedly of benefit to remove as little of the vegetable as necessary. It is possible to buy special Japanese vegetable scrubbers and I recommend their use whenever possible. The skin of vegetables is almost always nutritious and high in fibre, is usually quite colourful and can add interesting texture to your salad.

Some root vegetables which do require peeling will either require immediate dressing or placing in water acidulated with a little lemon juice or vinegar in order to prevent discoloration.

To blanch or not to blanch is a frequently debated question. Many people contend that lightly blanching some vegetables has the advantage of making them more digestible and improving their flavour. I tend to agree with this argument when applied to courgettes, cauliflower and French beans.

While cutting salad leaves might spoil them, cutting vegetables can make all the difference to the appearance of a salad. They should be cut to a uniform size, though not necessarily into the same shape and certainly not into such tiny pieces that the character of the vegetable is lost. The shape of the vegetable will normally dictate the type of cut that should be made. Long round shapes such as cucumber are normally sliced in rounds; globe shaped vegetables such as tomatoes can be sliced or cut into wedges and others such as peppers lend themselves to strip cutting. Against this is the julienne style of preparation, where the vegetable is cut into matchstick sized strips. Carrots, turnip and celery are particularly attractive served this way. Best results are achieved by careful use of a sharp knife but a reasonable result may be obtained by using a food processor.

Presentation

The choice of dish is of course of paramount importance in the successful presentation of your salad. Wooden bowls are ideal for green leafy salads, but shallow dishes or even oval platters are more attractive for the presentation of less bulky salads such as tomato and basil vinaigrette or Ceviche.

I very much enjoy finding attractive or unusual plates and dishes in local antique shops which make such a difference to the appearance of a salad.

Salad Starters

Egg and anchovy salad

Egg and anchovy salad

Serves 4

A piquant first course which I like to serve with thinly sliced
wholewheat bread.

4 hard-boiled eggs, sliced
1 tablespoon capers
1 tablespoon chopped gherkins
4 large tomatoes, sliced
4 tablespoons French dressing (see page 175)
2 teaspoons tomato purée
1 teaspoon clear honey
1 tablespoon chopped basil
50-g (1¾-oz) can anchovies, drained

Arrange the eggs on 4 plates and sprinkle with the capers and
gherkins. Arrange the tomato slices slightly overlapping the
eggs.

Place the French dressing, tomato purée, honey and herbs in
a bowl and mix together thoroughly, then pour a little over each
salad.

Slice the anchovies in half lengthways, and arrange lattice
fashion on top of the tomatoes.

Scandinavian salad

Serves 4

If you have ever visited Denmark or Sweden you will have discovered that the traditional smörgasbord frequently consists of herrings served raw, cooked or pickled, in more variations than you would have believed possible.

I think that this salad is one of the most delicious. The sharp, sour taste of the herring is complemented by the sweetness of the apple and they blend together delightfully in this creamy dill-flavoured dressing.

2 red-skinned apples, quartered and cored.
1 tablespoon lemon juice
250g (8oz) pickled herrings
1 onion, thinly sliced
1 dill pickle, thinly sliced
150ml (¼ pint) smetana*
freshly ground black pepper
1 tablespoon chopped fresh dill

Slice the apples thinly into a bowl, sprinkle with the lemon juice and toss to coat the apple and prevent discoloration.

Cut the herrings across into strips and add to the bowl with the onion and dill pickle.

Mix the smetana with the pepper and dill, then pour this over the salad and toss until coated. Spoon on to individual shallow dishes and serve with thinly sliced wholewheat bread.

Scallops ceviche

Serves 4

This refreshing and unusual dish would be ideal if you were planning a gourmet meal for a special occasion. The recipe originated in South America, where they have a unique method of marinating fish in lime or lemon juice, which gives it the opaque appearance of having been cooked. This does not apply only to scallops; any firm, white fish would suffice. Monkfish, for instance, would be a particularly good substitute.

The lovely smell and taste of coriander is typical of many Mexican dishes, and it certainly enhances this most impressive first course.

8 large scallops
juice of 3 limes or lemons
2 tablespoons chopped fresh coriander
4 tablespoons olive oil
2 spring onions, sliced diagonally
2 tomatoes, skinned and chopped
black pepper
1 avocado pear

Scrape the scallops from their shells, pull off the beard-like fringe, the intestinal thread, and cut off the coral. Wash them and dry thoroughly. Cut the white part into thin slices and place in a bowl with the corals. Pour over the lime juice, mix in the coriander and leave to marinate overnight.

Drain off 4 tablespoons of the lime juice and reserve.

Stir the oil, onions, tomato and pepper into the scallops until they are well coated.

Halve, peel and slice the avocado and brush the slices with the reserved lime juice.

Arrange the ceviche on individual serving plates and garnish with the avocado slices.

Salade tiède

Serves 4

This salad (the name means, literally, 'warm salad') is popular in France, where it is often served as a first course.

The sizzling pieces of chicken liver should still be lightly pink inside. You can use any wine vinegar, but a raspberry-flavoured variety gives the dish a special tang. As you toss the spinach with the hot liver, oil and vinegar it will begin to wilt slightly as the whole becomes warm – delicious!

175g (6oz) tender young spinach leaves
small head radicchio*
50g (2oz) walnuts
3 tablespoons olive oil
250g (8oz) chicken livers, cut into slices
3 tablespoons raspberry wine vinegar
salt and freshly ground pepper

Trim the stalks from the spinach, tear into pieces and place in a bowl. Tear the radicchio into pieces and add to the spinach. Sprinkle the walnuts over. Heat the oil in a frying pan, add the livers and fry for 3 to 4 minutes. Tip on to the salad.

Add the vinegar to the pan and stir to dissolve any juices, then pour over the salad, seasoning to taste with the salt and pepper. Toss thoroughly and serve immediately.

Sushi

Serves 6

Sushi are Japanese picnic foods, but I like to serve them as a first course. The Japanese pay particular attention to the garnish of their foods – tomato flowers, spring onion tassels or radish chrysanthemums all look very pretty served with sushi.

Sushi are very easy to make. The prepared rice mixture is placed on little bamboo sushi mats to facilitate rolling into shape.

175g (6oz) brown rice, washed
600ml (1 pint) water
2 tablespoons rice vinegar or cider vinegar
2 teaspoons clear honey
1 tablespoon shoyu*

FILLING
3 spring onions, sliced lengthways into strips
25g (1oz) peeled prawns
2 teaspoons horseradish relish
2 sheets nori*

GARNISH
Tomato flowers, radish chrysanthemums or spring onion tassels
(see pages 16–17)

Place the rice in a pan of boiling, salted water, cover and simmer gently for 35 to 40 minutes, until all the water has been absorbed. Mix the vinegar, honey and shoyu together, then pour over the rice. Mix well together and leave to cool.

Crisp one sheet of nori by passing it quickly over a flame, so that it turns green. Be careful not to scorch it. Put a sushi mat on the table and lay the nori on top of it. Place half the rice over the nori, spreading it evenly to the edges in a 5-mm (¼-inch) thick layer, leaving a border of about 2.5cm (1 inch) at the top end.

Arrange half the spring onions and prawns on the rice at one end and spread a little horseradish relish over the top. Roll up the nori into a cylinder shape, using the sushi mat. The plain nori at the end will stick and hold the roll in position. Remove the mat, then repeat with the remaining ingredients to make a second roll.

Using a sharp knife, cut each roll into 1.5-cm (¾-inch) thick slices. Lay, cut side downwards, on individual plates and garnish with the chosen vegetable.

Asparagus mayonnaise

Serves 4

When fresh asparagus is in season there is no better way to serve it than perfectly plain, with a home-made mayonnaise or vinaigrette dressing. Delicious!

500g (1lb) asparagus
salt
3 tablespoons mayonnaise (see page 177)
2 tablespoons yogurt

Cut the asparagus stalks to a uniform length, tie in bundles and place, standing upright, in a deep pan of boiling salted water. Take a large piece of foil and make a lid, doming it over the tips, so that the heads cook in the steam. Thin asparagus spears will take 15 minutes to cook; thicker stems will take up to 30 minutes.

Drain very carefully, then arrange on individual serving dishes and leave to cool.

Mix the mayonnaise with the yogurt to lighten it slightly, and spoon a little on to each plate.

VARIATION:

Asparagus vinaigrette

Spoon 1 tablespoon of vinaigrette dressing over each plate of asparagus while still warm. Cool before serving.

Artichoke with herb dressing

Serves 4

A vegetable, looking like a flower and tasting as succulent as any fruit, artichoke is certainly not for the quick snack but the choice for a relaxed and leisurely lunch or evening meal.

To accompany this paragon of vegetables choose French dressing (see page 175) or my own favourite, this delicious herb dressing.

4 globe artichokes, washed

HERB DRESSING
150ml (¼ pint) yogurt
1 clove garlic, crushed
1 tablespoon cider vinegar
1 teaspoon clear honey
salt and pepper
2 tablespoons chopped parsley
1 tablespoon chopped mint
1 tablespoon chopped olives

Trim the points of the leaves square with scissors and cut off the stalk to level the base.

Place in a large pan of boiling salted water and cook for 40 minutes or until a leaf can be pulled out easily. Drain well and allow to cool.

Pull out the central leaves, which are tinged with mauve, and carefully scrape out the choke, which is inedible.

Place all the dressing ingredients in an electric blender or food processor and blend until smooth.

Pour a little dressing over the *fond* or bottom of each artichoke and serve on individual dishers. Hand the remaining dressing separately.

Artichoke and Parma salad

Serves 4

I try to avoid the use of tinned products, but joyfully make an exception in the case of artichoke hearts. Delicious – especially when teamed with Parma ham.

397-g (14-oz) can artichoke hearts, drained
2 slices Parma ham
3 tablespoons French dressing (see page 175)
8 black olives, halved and stoned
1 tablespoon chopped parsley

Cut the artichoke hearts in half and arrange on a shallow serving dish.

Cut the ham into thin strips and lay over the artichokes. Pour the dressing evenly over the salad, then arrange the olives over the top. Sprinkle with the parsley and serve.

Celeriac remoulade

Serves 4

Every French delicatessen displays this gorgeous salad, which transforms the simplest wayside picnic into a memorable occasion.

This useful winter root vegetable is not used enough in Britain, which is a shame, as it has a fine flavour. Apart from using it blanched, as in this salad, it can be grated raw and tossed in a vinaigrette dressing and is also delicious cooked and mashed with potato to make a light mousseline.

500g (1lb) celeriac, peeled
4 tablespoons smetana*
2 tablespoons mayonnaise (see page 177)
2 tablespoons Dijon mustard
1 tablespoon chopped parsley

Cut the celeriac into strips measuring 3.5cm by 3mm (1½ inches by ⅛ inch), then blanch in boiling water for 2 minutes. Do not overcook the celeriac or it will lose its crispness. Drain well and leave to cool.

Mix the smetana with the mayonnaise and mustard, then pour over the celeriac and mix together thoroughly.

Turn into a shallow serving dish and sprinkle with parsley.

Avocado and tomato in yogurt

Serves 4

This refreshing salad is excellent to serve with spicy food, and one which I rather like to serve with barbecues.

1 large avocado pear, halved and stoned
300ml (½ pint) natural yogurt
2 tablespoons chopped basil
salt and freshly ground black pepper
4 large tomatoes, skinned and cut into chunks

Peel the avocado, cut into chunks and put in a bowl with the yogurt, basil and salt and pepper to taste.

Add the tomatoes and mix all together thoroughly.

Insalata tricolore

Serves 4

I first tasted this salad in an Italian restaurant at the Henley Festival and have served it frequently since. It is almost as attractive to look at as it is tasty to eat. Use good-sized plates to achieve the maximum effect.

1 avocado pear, halved and stoned
4 tablespoons French dressing (see page 175)
2 large tomatoes, sliced
125g (4oz) mozzarella cheese, thinly sliced
2 tablespoons chopped basil

Carefully remove the outer shells from the avocado halves.

Slice the avocado lengthways and dip each slice into the dressing to prevent it from going brown.

Arrange overlapping slices down one side of each individual plate. Arrange similar overlapping slices of tomato beside the avocado, and then repeat with the mozzarella. Spoon the remaining dressing over each salad and then spinkle with the basil.

Avocado with mozzarella vinaigrette

Serves 4

As avocados become more and more widely appreciated, interest in various ways of serving them increases. One addition with popular appeal is cheese, and a finishing touch of chopped basil, with its exciting aroma and flavour, creates a dish which is guaranteed to tempt the most jaded appetite!

2 avocado pears, halved and stoned
1 tablespoon lemon juice
250g (8oz) mozzarella cheese, sliced
3 tablespoons olive oil
1 tablespoon chopped basil
salt and black pepper

Peel each avocado, halve and cut lengthways into slices, then brush the slices lightly with lemon juice. Arrange the slices alternately with the mozzarella on individual plates, in a fan shape. Pour over the olive oil, sprinkle with basil, salt and pepper.

Avocado and cottage cheese salad

Serves 4

The combination of avocado and cottage cheese is one of my firm favourites. I usually serve the mixture on a bed of sliced tomatoes to create a more colourful and attractive finishing touch. This salad also makes a delightful, and easily prepared, light meal, accompanied by fresh crusty wholewheat bread.

4 tomatoes, sliced
1 avocado pear, halved and stoned
175g (6oz) cottage cheese
2 tablespoons chopped chives
freshly ground black pepper
2 teaspoons lemon juice

Arrange the tomatoes overlapping on 4 individual plates. Peel the avocado pear, cut into chunks and place in a bowl with the cheese and chives. Season with a little black pepper and lemon juice, and mix together so that the avocado is well coated.

Divide the mixture between the four plates, arranging it on top of the tomato slices.

Two-pear salad

Serves 4

An interesting way of serving avocado pear. You can buy offcuts of prosciutto ham for this recipe, as it is chopped up finely in the dressing.

2 William pears
1 tablespoon lemon juice
2 avocado pears, halved and stoned
*4 tablespoons smetana**
2 tablespoons chopped prosciutto ham
1 teaspoon lemon juice
1 tablespoon milk
freshly ground black pepper
4 sprigs chervil

Peel, quarter and core the William pears, slice them lengthways and brush with lemon juice. Slice the avocados lengthways, then arrange on 4 individual plates, interleaving them alternately with the William pear slices.

Mix the smetana with the prosciutto ham, lemon juice, milk and black pepper. Spoon the dressing across the middle of the pears and garnish with chervil sprigs.

Crudités with avocado dip

Serves 4

A lovely, summery first course. I often serve this before a barbecue, so that the guests have something tasty to nibble at leisure whilst enjoying the aroma of the main course to follow.

2 ripe avocado pears
2 tablespoons lemon juice
1 tablespoon grated onion
½ teaspoon Worcester sauce
5 tablespoons natural yogurt
salt and pepper

CRUDITÉS
4 carrots
4 sticks celery
1 green pepper, cored and seeded
1 red pepper, cored and seeded
½ small cauliflower

Halve the avocados and remove the stones. Scoop the flesh into a blender and add the remaining ingredients. Blend until smooth, then turn into a serving bowl.

Cut the carrots, celery and peppers into matchstick pieces, and break the cauliflower into florets.

Place the bowl of dip on a large platter and surround with alternating piles of vegetables.

Guacamole

Serves 4

Guacamole is very popular in Mexico, where it originates. I recommend serving it with corn chips or wholewheat toast.

Avocado will turn brown very quickly when exposed to air, so, if you want to prepare the dish early to keep for an hour or two, it's best to cover tightly with clingfilm. The discoloured surface can be stirred in just before serving.

This is a particularly good way to use avocados that have become too soft to serve halved or sliced.

2 ripe avocado pears
juice of one lime
1 clove garlic, crushed
3 spring onions, finely chopped
2 tomatoes, skinned, seeded and chopped
1 tablespoon chopped fresh coriander
. salt and black pepper

Halve the avocados and remove the stones. Scoop the flesh into a bowl and mash with the lime juice.

Add the remaining ingredients with salt and pepper to taste, then mix together thoroughly.

Turn into a small bowl and serve.

Avocado and prawn salad

Serves 4

One of the happiest combinations, avocado and prawns, with the addition of a little tomato, all tossed in a creamy tomato dressing and decorated with sprigs of fennel.

2 avocado pears
175g (6oz) prawns
3 tomatoes, skinned
6 tablespoons tomato cream dressing (see page 184)
4 sprigs fennel

Cut the avocado pears in half and remove the stones. Peel off the skin, the cut the flesh into chunks and place in a bowl with the prawns. Cut each tomato into 8 wedges and add to the bowl. Pour over the dressing and toss thoroughly until all the ingredients are well coated. Spoon into individual serving dishes and garnish each with a sprig of fennel.

Tropical prawns

Serves 8

Rather an expensive first course, but a worthwhile treat for the discerning palate.

Use fairly large plates so that the pear and paw paw slices can be well fanned out, for maximum effect.

2 avocado pears, halved and stoned
*1 paw paw, halved and seeded**
2 tablespoons French dressing (see page 175)
250g (8oz) peeled prawns
6 tablespoons tomato cream dressing (see page 184)
sprigs of dill to garnish

Peel the avocado and paw paw thinly and cut each lengthways into thin slices.

Lay alternate slices of paw paw and avocado on 8 individual plates, arranging them in a fan shape. Brush the exposed avocado with the French dressing to prevent discoloration.

Place the prawns in a bowl, spoon over the tomato cream dressing, and mix well. Spoon some of the dressed prawns in a line across the sliced fruit and decorate each serving with a sprig of dill.

South Seas salad

Serves 4

A really exotic salad with exciting flavours that complement each other beautifully, and are pleasantly sharpened by the lime dressing.

1 avocado pear, halved and stoned
3 tablespoons lime dressing (see page 177)
1 paw paw, halved and seeded
2 kiwi fruits, peeled
1 tablespoon sesame seeds, toasted

Peel the avocado pear, cut into quarters then into diagonal slices. Place in a bowl with the lime dressing and toss to coat completely, so that they do not discolour.

Peel the paw paw, cut into 4 quarters and then into diagonal slices and place in the bowl with the avocado. Slice the kiwi fruits thinly, add to the other fruits and toss again to coat completely.

Divide between 4 individual serving dishes, and sprinkle with the sesame seeds.

Palm hearts and paw paw vinaigrette

Serves 8

A really impressive first course to serve at a dinner party. The colours complement each other, as do the subtly intriguing flavours. Pine nuts are the seeds from the stone pine, native to the Mediterranean, and have a soft texture. I think the flavour is much improved if they are lightly toasted under the grill.

2 397-g (14-oz) cans palm hearts, drained*
1 paw paw, halved and seeded*
120ml (4fl oz) lemon dressing (see page 176)
2 tablespoons chopped chervil
2 tablespoons pine kernels, toasted

Slice each palm heart into 4 lengthways and arrange on 8 individual dishes.

Peel the paw paw thinly and cut lengthways into thin slices. Lay crossways over the palm hearts, overlapping slightly.

Spoon a little dressing over each plate and sprinkle with the chervil and pine nuts.

Watermelon and mint vinaigrette

Serves 4

A really delicious and refreshing salad, ideal to serve with an *al fresco* meal in summer or as a cool side dish with a curry.

625g (1¼lb) watermelon, cut into thin wedges
¼ cucumber
2 tablespoons chopped mint
2 tablespoons lemon dressing (see page 176)

Remove the seeds from the watermelon and discard. Carefully cut away the skin, and then cut the melon flesh into slices and place in a bowl.

Slice the cucumber, cut the slices in half and place in the bowl with the mint and dressing. Toss well to coat, then transfer to a shallow serving dish.

Watermelon and strawberry vinaigrette

Serves 4

An exquisite salad, both in appearance and flavour, and a very refreshing opening course which I first served to a large family party at an *al fresco* lunch.

The summer's day was perfect: warm sun, gentle soft breeze perfumed with roses. We spread the long tables with white cloths under the fruit trees in the garden, and started a memorable meal with this delightful dish.

> *500g (1lb) watermelon, cut into wedges*
> *125g (4oz) strawberries, sliced*
> *1 tablespoon chopped mint*
> *125g (4oz) cucumber*
> *1 tablespoon lemon dressing (see page 176)*

Pick out the seeds from the watermelon and discard. Cut off the skin, then slice the melon diagonally into 1-cm (½-inch) pieces.

Place the melon in a bowl with the strawberries and sprinkle with the mint.

Slice the cucumber and then cut in half again and add to the bowl.

Pour the dressing over the salad and toss until well coated. Leave for 30 minutes for the flavours to combine and then serve in individual glass dishes.

Melon and prawn vinaigrette

Serves 6

A summery and very refreshing first course to serve during the melon season. If you prefer you can reserve the melon shells and serve the salad in them.

2 small Ogen melons
4 tomatoes, skinned
250g (8oz) prawns
1 tablespoon chopped dill
6 tablespoons vinaigrette dressing (see page 175)

Cut the melons in half and discard the seeds. Scoop the flesh into balls, using a melon baller, or cut into cubes.

Cut each tomato into 8 wedges and place in a bowl with the melon, prawns and dill.

Pour over the dressing, toss well and spoon into individual serving dishes.

Tomato and pesto vinaigrette

Serves 6

A simple first course to make whenever you can gather together enough basil to make the vinaigrette.

500g (1lb) Marmande tomatoes
25g (1oz) black olives, halved and stoned
6 tablespoons pesto vinaigrette (see page 185)
75g (3oz) feta cheese

Slice the tomatoes, then cut the slices into halves. Place in a bowl with the olives, pour in the *pesto* vinaigrette and toss until well coated.

Leave for one hour for the flavours to mingle, then turn into a serving dish.

Just before serving, crumble the cheese over the top.

Gazpacho jalea

Serves 6

An intriguing variation of the refreshing and world-renowned Spanish soup. The jelly retains the soup's sharp tang and delicious flavour. To complete the dish it is a good idea to dice double the quantity of vegetables and put half aside to be tossed in vinaigrette and used as a garnish around the individual jellies.

450ml (¾ pint) tomato juice
1 clove garlic, crushed
1 teaspoon clear honey
1 tablespoon cider vinegar
3 tablespoons olive oil
4 tablespoons cold water
15g (½oz) gelatine
¼ cucumber
3 tomatoes, peeled and chopped
½ green pepper, cored, seeded and chopped
2 spring onions, chopped
salt and pepper

Mix the tomato juice, garlic, honey, vinegar and oil together in a bowl. Place the water in a small saucepan and sprinkle in the gelatine. Leave to soak for 5 minutes, then heat very gently and pour into the tomato mixture.

Cut 6 slices of cucumber and set aside. Cut the remaining cucumber into dice and add to the tomato juice mixture, together with the tomatoes, green pepper and spring onions, then season to taste.

Pour into six ramekins and place in the refrigerator to set.

Dip the ramekins into hot water for an instant to loosen, then turn them on to individual serving plates and garnish each with a cucumber slice.

Brie and tomato salad

Serves 4

Although the rind of Brie is edible, you may prefer to remove it for this recipe.

With or without the rind, Brie and Tomato Salad is delicious served with plenty of hot garlic bread.

250g (8oz) Brie
4 Marmande tomatoes
2 tablespoons chopped basil
4 tablespoons French dressing (see page 175)

Cut the Brie into chunks and place in a bowl with the remaining ingredients. Toss thoroughly and serve on small individual dishes.

Salade de chèvre grillée

Serves 4

An unusual first course which is a great favourite with my family and friends – hot goat's cheese and cold, crisp salad. The exciting aroma of toasting cheese, oregano and nuts is a taste bud titillator – a promising start to any meal!

175-g (6-oz) roll chèvre
½ teaspoon oregano
15g (1oz) hazelnut, chopped
1 bunch watercress
few curly endive leaves
2 tablespoons French dressing (see page 175)

Cut the *chèvre* into 12 pieces and lay on a piece of foil on a grill pan. Sprinkle with the oregano and hazelnuts.

Wash the watercress, shake dry and break into sprigs, then

place in a bowl. Tear the endive leaves into pieces and add to the bowl with the dressing. Toss thoroughly and then arrange on 4 individual plates.

Place the *chèvre* under a hot grill and grill for 1 to 2 minutes until the nuts brown and the cheese begins to melt. Lift 3 slices on to the watercress salad on each plate and serve immediately.

Mediterranean pepper salad

Serves 4

You'll find variations of this salad throughout the Mediterranean. It is important to cook the vegetables until the skins are black, so that you get that delicious smoky flavour and soft, tender vegetables.

1 aubergine
1 red pepper
1 yellow pepper
1 green pepper
4 tablespoons garlic dressing (see page 175)
2 tablespoons chopped parsley

Cut the aubergine in half and lay, cut side downwards, on a greased baking sheet. Grill slowly for about 20 minutes until the skin is blackened, and the flesh soft to touch.

Halve the peppers and grill these in the same way for about 10 minutes.

Cool the vegetables a little then peel off the skins, discarding the seeds from the peppers.

Cut the flesh into strips and place in a bowl. Pour over the garlic dressing, add the parsley and toss to coat the vegetables.

Pepperonata

Serves 6

I particularly like peppers, and think this is a delicious way to serve them. I usually make twice the quantity needed, as it is so useful to have some left over for lunches during the week.

3 tablespoons olive oil
1 onion, sliced
1 large yellow pepper, halved, seeded and sliced
1 large green pepper, halved, seeded and sliced
1 large red pepper, halved, seeded and sliced
2 cloves garlic, crushed
6 tomatoes, skinned and sliced
2 tablespoons chopped parsley
salt and pepper

Heat the oil in a heavy-based pan and fry the onion, peppers and garlic over a gentle heat for about 15 minutes, stirring occasionally.

Add the tomatoes, parsley and seasoning to taste and cook for a further 5 minutes. Leave to cool, then serve in individual dishes.

Courgettes provençales

Serves 4

Simply delicious! Serve with chunky slices of wholemeal bread.

500g (1lb) courgettes, topped and tailed
3 tablespoons olive oil
1 onion, chopped
2 cloves garlic, crushed
4 tomatoes, skinned and chopped
25g (1oz) black olives, halved and stoned
salt and freshly ground black pepper

Cut each courgette into ½-cm (¼-inch) thick slices, lengthways.

Heat the oil in a large frying pan and cook the onion and courgettes over a gentle heat for 10 to 15 minutes, stirring occasionally until softened.

Add the garlic, tomatoes, olives and seasoning to taste, cover with foil and cook for a further 5 to 8 minutes. Allow to cool, then arrange the courgettes on a serving dish and spoon over the tomatoes and olives.

Leeks niçoise

Serves 4

It is surprising that the leek, a good vegetable with a very distinctive flavour, is not more widely used. Beyond being chopped up and added to the stewpot, or covered with cheese and breadcrumbs, it seems to be neglected. I find that leeks have great scope, and one successful variation is as the basic ingredient of this savoury and memorable salad.

8 thin leeks
salt
2 tablespoons olive oil
1 clove garlic, crushed
3 tomatoes, chopped
25g (1oz) black olives, halved and stoned
1 tablespoon chopped basil
1 tablespoon chopped parsley
freshly ground black pepper

Trim the leeks to about 15cm (6 inches), split in half lengthways and wash thoroughly under running water.

Tie in two bundles and cook the leeks in boiling, salted water for about 6 minutes until just tender, then drain well and remove the string.

Heat the oil in a shallow pan, add the garlic and cook for 1 minute. Add the tomatoes, olives, basil and parsley, season and bring to the boil. Add the leeks, cover with the sauce and simmer gently for 5 minutes.

Transfer the leeks to a serving dish and spoon the sauce over the top. Cool before serving.

Caponata

Serves 6

This is a traditional Sicilian salad. It has a piquant flavour reminiscent of sun-warmed earth and the tangy scent of sea and pines – in a word, the Mediterranean.

1 aubergine
salt
4 tablespoons olive oil
2 sticks celery, diced
1 onion, chopped
4 tomatoes, skinned and chopped
1 teaspoon tomato purée
50g (2oz) stoned green olives
1 tablespoon cider vinegar
1 teaspoon clear honey
1 tablespoon capers
2 tablespoons chopped parsley

Cut the aubergine into 1-cm (½-inch) cubes. Place in a colander, sprinkle with salt and leave for 30 minutes. Rinse well and pat dry with kitchen paper.

Heat 3 tablespoons of the oil in a frying pan and fry the aubergine and celery over a gentle heat for about 15 minutes, stirring frequently until beginning to brown. Turn into a bowl.

Add the remaining oil to the pan and fry the onion until softened. Add the remaining ingredients, together with the aubergine mixture, stir well, cover and cook for a further 10 minutes.

Leave to cool, then turn on to a serving dish and serve with crusty bread.

Ratatouille

Serves 6

I love ratatouille served cold as a first course, but prefer the vegetables to be more lightly cooked than they are in a traditional ratatouille. You can use either green or red peppers, but the latter give the dish a brilliant, and very appetizing, flash of colour.

1 small aubergine, sliced
salt
4 tablespoons oil
1 onion, sliced
1 red pepper, cored, seeded and sliced
250g (8oz) courgettes, sliced
2 cloves garlic, crushed
freshly ground black pepper
1 teaspoon chopped marjoram
4 tomatoes, skinned and sliced

Place the aubergine in a colander, sprinkle with salt and leave to soak for 30 minutes. This will remove the indigestible juices and also reduce the amount of oil necessary for frying. Rinse well and pat dry with kitchen paper.

Heat half the oil in a frying pan and cook the aubergine on both sides until it starts to turn brown. Remove from the pan and place in a bowl.

Add the remaining oil to the pan and fry the onion until softened, then add the pepper and courgettes and cook for about 8 minutes, stirring occasionally until softened.

Add the garlic, seasoning to taste and the marjoram, and cook for a further 2 minutes. Add to the aubergine in the bowl with the tomatoes.

Mix well and then allow to cool, before serving in individual shallow dishes.

Turkish aubergine salad

Serves 4 to 6

Mezze are part of a way of life in the Middle East. Many different little dishes are offered together as part of an hors d'oeuvre, so you are able to sample a great variety of different foods at one sitting. Turkish Aubergine Salad is a typical *mezze* and one of my favourites, which is why I've suggested you make rather more than would normally be served.

2 aubergines
salt
4 tablespoons olive oil
1 green pepper, halved, seeded and chopped
2 cloves garlic, crushed
4 tomatoes, skinned and chopped
2 tablespoons chopped parsley
300ml (½ pint) yogurt
salt and freshly ground black pepper

Cut the aubergines into 1-cm (½-inch) cubes. Place in a colander, sprinkle with salt and leave for 30 minutes. Rinse well and dry with kitchen paper.

Heat the oil in a frying pan, add the aubergines and green pepper and fry for 10 to 15 minutes, stirring occasionally, until softened. Add the garlic and tomatoes and cook for a further 2 minutes.

Turn into a bowl and allow to cool, then add the parsley, yogurt and seasoning to taste. Stir together gently and transfer to a shallow serving dish.

Yogurt and aubergine salad

Serves 4 to 6

Aubergines absorb a lot of oil during frying. To avoid this and to rid them of their indigestible juices too, it is best to *dégorger* them before use. To do this you simply sprinkle them with salt and leave them to drain for 30 minutes. The fresh mint-flavoured yogurt counteracts the richness of the fried aubergines.

2 aubergines, sliced
salt
6 tablespoons olive oil
3 cloves garlic, crushed
300ml (½ pint) yogurt
2 tablespoons chopped mint
salt and freshly ground black pepper

Place the aubergines in a colander, sprinkle with salt, and leave to drain for 30 minutes. Rinse well and pat dry with kitchen paper.

Heat the oil in a pan and fry the aubergines on each side until golden. Add the garlic and fry for about 1 minute, then remove to a plate and allow to cool.

Mix the yogurt with the mint and season to taste. Spoon some yogurt into the bottom of a shallow serving dish, arrange the aubergines on top, then pour over the remaining yogurt.

Aubergine salad

Serves 6

This very rich Middle Eastern salad makes an excellent first course, although I also find it enjoyable eaten as a supper dish, served with wholemeal bread and a green salad.

2 aubergines, sliced
salt
3 tablespoons olive oil
2 cloves garlic, crushed
397-g (14-oz) can tomatoes, chopped
2 tablespoons chopped parsley
freshly ground black pepper

GARNISH
onion rings
1 tablespoon pine nuts, browned
1 tablespoon chopped parsley

Place the aubergines in a colander, sprinkle with salt and leave for 30 minutes to remove the indigestible juices. Rinse well and pat dry with kitchen paper.

Heat the oil in a pan and fry the aubergines on each side until golden. Add the garlic and fry for one minute, then add the tomatoes and parsley. Season to taste, cover and simmer for 10 minutes, stirring occasionally.

Allow to cool, covered, then place in a shallow serving dish. Place the onion rings over the top and sprinkle with the pine nuts and parsley.

Taramasalata

Serves 4

Traditionally, Taramasalata is prepared by hand in a pestle and mortar. However, it is much quicker and the result possibly much better if the whole thing is blended in a food processor. Adjust the quantity of lemon juice and oil to taste.

75g (3oz) wholewheat bread
3 tablespoons water
juice of 1 lemon
75g (3oz) smoked cod's roe
2 cloves garlic, chopped
3 tablespoons olive oil

Place the bread in a small bowl with the water and lemon juice, pressing down well to submerge, and leave to soak for 10 minutes.

Scrape into a food processor and add the cod's roe, garlic and oil. Blend until very smooth, scraping down the sides if necessary.

Turn into a bowl and serve with olives and wholewheat pitta bread.

Hummus bi tahini

Serves 10

One of the most popular *mezze* from the Middle East, and now becoming more widely known in Britain. It is always useful to have a bowl of hummus in the refrigerator to dip into for a quick snack with crudités, so I make quite a large quantity at a time.

250g (8oz) chick peas, soaked overnight
1 teaspoon turmeric
4 tablespoons tahini*
3 cloves garlic
juice of 1 to 2 lemons
salt and freshly ground pepper
paprika pepper to garnish

Drain the chick peas, place in a large pan with the turmeric and cover with cold water. Bring to the boil, cover and cook for about one hour, until the chick peas are soft. The cooking time will vary depending on the quality and age of the chick peas. Drain and reserve about 300ml (½ pint) of the cooking water.

Place the chick peas in a food processor with the tahini, garlic and the juice of 1 lemon, also a little salt and pepper, with enough of the reserved liquid to blend to a soft, creamy paste.

Taste and adjust the seasoning, adding more garlic or lemon until you achieve the right balance. Turn into a shallow bowl, sprinkle with the paprika and serve with wholewheat pitta bread.

Creamed sesame salad

Serves 6

A very popular hors d'oeuvre in the Middle East, where it is served with Arab bread.

> *3 good sprigs parsley*
> *1 clove garlic*
> *150ml (¼ pint) tahini paste**
> *225ml (8 fl oz) natural yogurt*
> *3 tablespoons lemon juice*
> *salt*
> *freshly ground black pepper*
> *50g (2oz) ground almonds*
> *1 tablespoon chopped parsley to garnish*

Place the parsley and garlic in a food processor and chop finely. Add the tahini paste, yogurt and lemon juice with a little salt and pepper. Process until smooth, then taste for seasoning and add a little more lemon juice or salt if necessary.

Turn into a bowl and mix with the ground almonds. Place in a shallow serving dish, sprinkle with the parsley and serve with pitta bread or sticks of raw vegetables.

Side Salads

Apple and watercress vinaigrette

Beanshoot and mangetout vinaigrette

Serves 4 to 6

A very pretty salad with an oriental flavour, easily prepared and guaranteed to bring forth compliments for the cook! If the mangetouts are really small then they are even more delicious left raw.

250g (8oz) mangetout peas
2 red peppers, cored and seeded
175g (6oz) beanshoots
2 tablespoons sesame seeds, roasted
6 tablespoons ginger dressing (see page 181)

Top and tail the mangetouts and, if large, cut in half diagonally. Blanch in boiling, salted water for 3 minutes, rinse in cold water and drain.

Slice the red peppers finely and place in a bowl with the cooled mangetouts, the beanshoots, sesame seeds and dressing. Toss thoroughly and transfer to a shallow serving dish.

Beanshoot and orange salad

Serves 4 to 6

A very crisp salad. Fresh and easy to eat, it can be served at any meal and you can be happy that, while you are enjoying the delightful nutty taste of the sesame seeds, the crunchy beanshoots are doing you a power of good.

2 oranges
125g (4oz) beanshoots
1 bunch watercress, washed and sprigged
2 heads chicory
3 tablespoons French dressing (see page 175)
2 tablespoons sesame seeds, roasted

Peel the oranges, removing all the pith, and cut into segments. Place in a bowl with the beanshoots and watercress.

Cut the chicory into 1.25-cm (½-inch) wide diagonal slices and add to the bowl.

Toss well in the dressing, transfer to a salad bowl, and sprinkle with the sesame seeds.

Fennel and alfalfa salad

Serves 4

Alfalfa was one of the first plants to be cultivated. It is a sprout which grows from seed in just a few days, and is very well worth the little effort it takes to grow it at home, a pleasant task which children will often undertake with enthusiasm. (See page 26 for instructions on sprouting seeds.)

2 fennel bulbs
3 tablespoons chopped parsley
4 tablespoons lemon dressing (see page 176)
125g (4oz) alfalfa sprouts
1 tablespoon sesame seeds, toasted

Trim the stalks, base and tough outer leaves from the fennel. Cut the bulbs in half, then slice very finely.

Place in a bowl with the parsley and dressing, toss thoroughly and leave to marinate for about 1 hour.

Pull the alfalfa apart to loosen it, mix with the fennel, then transfer to a salad bowl and sprinkle with the sesame seeds.

Grape and almond coleslaw

Serves 6 to 8

The success of this salad depends very much on the cabbage being very finely shredded. I use a mandoline, which not only achieves the fine shredding but speeds up the process considerably.

The nuts give a gorgeous crunchiness, and using the smetana dressing instead of mayonnaise lowers the fat content and gives a much lighter and more pleasant result.

250g (8oz) black grapes
250g (8oz) Dutch cabbage, finely shredded
4 spring onions, thinly sliced
2 sticks celery, thinly sliced
50g (2oz) split almonds, browned
150ml (¼ pint) smetana dressing (see page 186)

Halve the grapes, remove the pips and place in a bowl with the cabbage. Add the remaining ingredients and toss the salad until well coated. Transfer to a salad bowl and serve.

Christmas coleslaw

Serves 6 to 8

This coleslaw will add colour to the festive Christmas table, and brighten the Boxing Day buffet!

The lovely green of Savoy cabbage contrasts beautifully with the carrot. It is a Christmas must in our family.

Caraway seeds can be substituted for the sesame seeds if you prefer.

1 Savoy cabbage
2 dessert apples, quartered and cored
6 tablespoons French dressing (see page 175)
3 carrots, peeled and grated
2 sticks celery, thinly sliced
1 tablespoon sesame seeds, toasted
2 tablespoons chopped parsley

Halve the cabbage, then cut away the larger stalks. Shred the cabbage very finely on a mandoline, or with a sharp knife, and place in a bowl.

Chop the apples, place in a bowl and pour over the dressing. Toss to coat completely so that they do not turn brown. Tip into the bowl of cabbage and add the carrots, celery, sesame seeds and parsley. Toss once again thoroughly.

Red cabbage and walnut salad

Serves 8

A colourful and crunchy salad, ideal to serve during winter months when other salad ingredients are in short supply.

It is also very good served with a yogurt dressing (see page 181), for a change.

350g (12oz) red cabbage
6 tablespoons French dressing (see page 175)
2 sticks celery, thinly sliced
2 dessert apples, quartered and cored
4 spring onions
50g (2oz) walnuts, roughly chopped

Shred the cabbage very finely, on a mandoline if you have one, or with a sharp knife. Place in a bowl, pour over the dressing and leave to marinate for 1 hour, tossing occasionally.

Add the celery, apples, onions and walnuts and toss thoroughly until coated with the dressing.

Chinese cabbage salad

Serves 4

Chinese cabbage, or Chinese leaves as it is sometimes called, makes a very useful salad ingredient during the winter months, when it is imported from Israel.

It has the advantage of remaining crisp and fresh in the refrigerator for up to a week, and can be used instead of those tasteless hothouse lettuces that go limp so quickly.

175g (6oz) Chinese cabbage
125g (4oz) beanshoots
1 bunch watercress, washed
6 tablespoons mustard dressing (see page 179)

Shred the cabbage finely and place in a salad bowl with the beanshoots. Break the watercress into sprigs, discarding any hairy stalks, and add to the bowl. Pour over the dressing and toss thoroughly.

Broccoli and avocado vinaigrette

Serves 6

You can use the purple sprouting, the purple hearting (resembling a purple cauliflower), or the calabrese varieties for this salad (see Broccoli, page 27). Be very careful not to overcook the broccoli, or it will lose the crispness that is so essential for this, or indeed, any salad.

350g (12oz) broccoli
salt
6 tablespoons French dressing (see page 175)
1 avocado, halved and stoned
1 red pepper, cored, seeded and thinly sliced
50g (2oz) roughly chopped hazelnuts, browned

Cut off the broccoli stalks and slice thinly, then divide the head into florets. Place the stalks into a little boiling, salted water and lay the florets over the top. Cover, and cook for 3 to 4 minutes. The heads will steam while the stalks cook in the water. Rinse under cold water, drain and place in a bowl with the dressing. Toss to coat and leave to cool.

Peel the avocado and cut into chunks. Add to the broccoli, together with the red pepper and hazelnuts. Toss thoroughly again to coat the avocado, and transfer to a serving dish.

Pear and Roquefort salad

Serves 4

The sweetness of the pear makes it a perfect partner for radicchio, which is sharp, and watercress, which is peppery.

I like this salad best served with a Roquefort dressing, but honey and lemon dressing (see page 176) makes a very pleasant alternative.

1 bunch watercress
6 radicchio leaves
2 pears
6 tablespoons Roquefort dressing (see page 184)

Wash the watercress thoroughly, shake dry and break into sprigs. Break the radicchio into manageable pieces and arrange together on individual plates.

Quarter and core the pears and cut into slices. Arrange half a pear over the salad on each plate, then coat with the Roquefort dressing.

Radicchio and Roquefort salad

Serves 6

Radicchio is a member of the chicory family; this particular variety originates in Italy. It has a decidedly sharp flavour which marries very well with Roquefort and toasted hazelnuts.

1 small head radicchio, washed
½ head curly endive, washed
1 bunch watercress, washed
50g (2oz) hazelnuts, browned
250g (8oz) Roquefort dressing (see page 184)

Break the radicchio and endive into manageable pieces and place in a bowl. Wash the watercress well, shake dry and break into sprigs, then add to the bowl with the hazelnuts.

Pour over the dressing and toss thoroughly to coat completely.

Salade frisée

Serves 4

Curly endive makes a very pretty and inviting salad. Although it may be a little more costly than the ordinary round lettuce, it keeps crisp and fresh much longer and there is so little waste that it is more economical in the long run.

½ head curly endive
½ small radicchio
50g (2oz) walnuts, chopped
4 tablespoons vinaigrette dressing (see page 175)

Tear the endive and radicchio into manageable pieces and place in a salad bowl. Add the walnuts and dressing and toss together thoroughly.

Salade mesclun

Serves 6

This is a salad from Provence, which originally made use of the wild herbs that grow so profusely in the hills. Nowadays it is made from a selection of many different cultivated salad plants, such as curly endive, Batavia, lamb's lettuce, radicchio, fennel and dandelion leaves.

One particular herb I always like to include if possible is rocket, which has a warm peppery flavour. Rocket is quite easy to grow but very rarely seen.

This is an extremely attractive salad.

½ head curly endive, washed
1 small head radicchio, washed
125g (4oz) lamb's lettuce, washed
few dandelion leaves (use only very young leaves), washed
½ bulb fennel, finely shredded
50g (2oz) walnuts, roughly chopped
few sprigs rocket (optional)
2 tablespoons chopped parsley
90ml (3 fl oz) vinaigrette dressing (see page 175)

Tear the endive and radicchio into manageable pieces and place in a salad bowl. Remove the roots from the lamb's lettuce and add to the bowl with the dandelion leaves, fennel, walnuts, rocket and parsley. Pour over the dressing and toss thoroughly.

Salade de pissenlits

Serves 4

Who but the French would give a flower, even a weed, such a name! There can be no truth in the old rumour, otherwise this salad would not be so widely popular in France.

It is essential to use only the young, tender dandelion leaves,

as the older ones will have become too tough and will have lost
their pleasant flavour.

I prefer to add fresh spinach leaves to this salad, as I find that
if it is made with dandelion leaves alone, the flavour is too
sharp. The crispy, fried bacon and rather bland egg also tend to
counteract any acidity.

50g (2oz) baby dandelion leaves
50g (2oz) tender spinach leaves
2 hard-boiled eggs, roughly chopped
125g (4oz) lean smoked bacon
1 clove garlic, crushed
2 teaspoons olive oil
2 tablespoons cider vinegar
salt and freshly ground pepper

Trim the leaves, wash and dry well, tear into pieces and place in
a salad bowl with the eggs.

Chop the bacon and fry with the garlic in the oil. Pour over
the salad, together with any oil, while still hot – and toss well.

Add the vinegar to the pan to dissolve any juices, and pour
over the salad, seasoning with salt and pepper. Toss once again
thoroughly and serve immediately.

Caesar salad

Serves 4 to 6

One of the most popular of the many salads originating in
America. Traditionally it is made with Cos lettuce, although any
crisp variety, such as Webb's Wonder or Iceberg, will suffice.

1 egg
1 clove garlic, crushed
2 tablespoons lemon juice
3 tablespoons olive oil
4 anchovy fillets, chopped finely
freshly ground black pepper
1 large Cos lettuce
2 hard-boiled eggs, roughly chopped
4 tablespoons freshly grated Parmesan cheese
3 slices wholewheat bread, crusts removed
4 tablespoons corn oil

Whisk together the raw egg, garlic, lemon juice, olive oil, anchovy fillets and black pepper to taste.

Tear the lettuce into manageable pieces and place it in a salad bowl with the chopped egg and cheese.

Cut the bread into 5-mm (¼-inch) cubes and fry in the corn oil until golden. Drain well on kitchen paper.

Pour the dressing over the salad and toss thoroughly, then sprinkle the croutons over the top.

Apple and watercress vinaigrette

Serves 4

A crisp, fresh salad, transformed from pleasant to delectable by the addition of toasted sesame seeds, and nasturtium flowers.

3 red-skinned dessert apples, quartered and cored
6 tablespoons lemon dressing (see page 176)
1 bunch watercress
4 sticks celery, thinly sliced
2 tablespoons sesame seeds, toasted
8 nasturtium flowers

Slice the apples thinly into a bowl, pour over the dressing and toss thoroughly to coat the apples so that they do not go brown.

Wash the watercress, shake dry and break into sprigs, then

add to the bowl with the celery and sesame seeds. Toss well once more, transfer to a salad bowl and garnish with the flowers.

Watercress and cucumber salad

Serves 4

A light, refreshing salad which would be a good choice to accompany a rather rich main course – roast duck, for instance, or roast goose.

1 bunch watercress, washed
¼ cucumber
1 tablespoon shoyu*
1 tablespoon cider vinegar
1 tablespoon finely chopped ginger
1 tablespoon sesame seeds, roasted

Break the watercress into sprigs, discarding any hairy stalks, and place in a bowl.

Slice the cucumber thinly, cut in half to form semicircles, and add to the watercress.

Mix the shoyu, vinegar and ginger together, then pour over the salad and toss thoroughly.

Transfer to a serving dish and sprinkle with the sesame seeds.

Nasturtium salad

Serves 4

Once you have stopped admiring the visual impact of this dish, you will be equally delighted with the peppery bite these attractive flowers give to any green salad.

Nasturtiums are well worth cultivating for leaf and flower and they will thrive in a window box, but if you are unable to grow them, worry not – I have seen them in some supermarkets!

1 bunch watercress
½ curly endive
250g (8oz) beanshoots
12 nasturtium flowers
6 tablespoons vinaigrette dressing (see page 175)

Wash the watercress well, shake dry and break into sprigs. Tear the endive into manageable pieces and place in a bowl with the watercress, beanshoots and flowers. Pour over the dressing and toss thoroughly. Turn into a salad bowl.

Watermelon and cress salad

Serves 4

A simple and refreshing salad to serve on hot, sunny days. The contrasting colours of the brilliant red watermelon, creamy chicory and bright green watercress look wonderful when displayed in a white salad bowl.

500g (1lb) watermelon, cut in wedges
2 heads chicory, sliced diagonally
1 bunch watercress, washed
2 tablespoons sesame seeds, roasted
2 tablespoons orange dressing (see page 177)

Remove the seeds from the watermelon, and discard. Cut the melon from the skin, then slice it diagonally into wedge shapes. Place in a bowl with the watercress, broken into small sprigs, and the remaining ingredients. Toss thoroughly, and serve in a shallow dish.

Chicory and avocado salad

Serves 4

Chicory is particularly useful, as it is available from autumn to spring when other salad ingredients are most scarce. Chicory will keep well in the chilling compartment of the refrigerator, wrapped in foil – it will become green and bitter on exposure to light. The slightly bitter flavour of the chicory blends well with the bland avocado and sweet orange.

3 heads chicory
1 avocado pear, halved and stoned
1 orange
2 tablespoons pumpkin seeds, toasted
4 tablespoons lemon vinaigrette dressing (see page 176)

Cut the chicory diagonally across into 1-cm (½-inch) slices and place in a salad bowl.

Peel the avocado and cut into slices. Remove the peel and pith from the orange and cut into segments, then place both in the salad bowl.

Add the pumpkin seeds, pour over the dressing, and toss well to coat.

Salads to Accompany
Main Meals

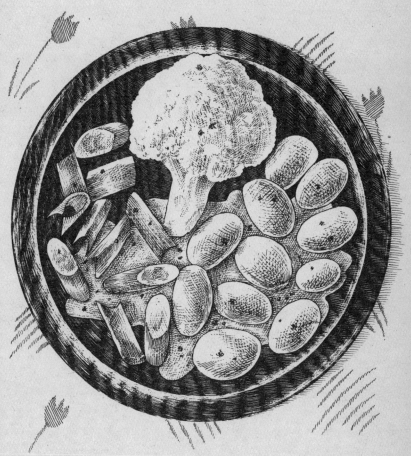

Broad bean and cauliflower salad

Hot potato salad

Serves 6

A boon if you have unexpected guests, this is a potato salad you can make at the last minute, as the potatoes don't have to be cooled. It is also very good served at barbecues, or any *al fresco* meal.

750g (1½lb) waxy potatoes, scrubbed
salt
1 onion, finely chopped
2 tablespoons chopped parsley
4 tablespoons French dressing (see page 175)
4 chive flowers

Cook the potatoes in boiling, salted water until tender. Drain well, chop roughly and place in a mixing bowl. Add the onion, parsley and dressing.

Mix thoroughly until well coated and transfer to a shallow serving dish. Separate the chive heads into individual flowers and sprinkle over the salad.

Curried potato salad

Serves 4

A mild curry-flavoured mayonnaise and fresh coriander give an appetizing piquancy to this nourishing salad.

500g (1lb) waxy potatoes, scrubbed
salt
3 hard-boiled eggs, chopped roughly
1 tablespoon fresh coriander, chopped
120ml (4 fl oz) curry mayonnaise (see page 178)

Cook the potatoes in boiling, salted water until tender. Drain well, chop roughly and leave to cool.

Place in a bowl with the eggs and coriander, pour over the dressing and mix together thoroughly.

Serve in a shallow dish.

Meaux potato salad

Serves 4

One of the simplest and yet most delicious potato salads I know. Its mildly hot flavour makes it ideal to serve with cold beef or ham.

500g (1lb) new potatoes, scrubbed
2 tablespoons French dressing (see page 175)
2 tablespoons Moutard de Meaux
150ml (¼ pint) smetana*

Cut the potatoes into even-sized pieces, place in a pan of boiling, salted water and cook for about 15 minutes, until tender. Drain well, place in a bowl, mix with the French dressing and leave to cool.

Mix the mustard and smetana together, then pour over the potatoes and toss gently but thoroughly. Transfer to a shallow serving dish.

Tomato and potato salad

Serves 4

This tomato and potato salad is made much tastier by the addition of nasturtium leaves. Nasturtiums are grown so easily in so many gardens and yet rarely recognized as a valuable salad ingredient. They have a strong peppery flavour which is particularly useful with blander vegetables.

500g (1lb) waxy potatoes
1 small onion, finely chopped
2 tablespoons French dressing (see page 175)
250g (8oz) tomatoes, skinned
8 nasturtium leaves, shredded
6 tablespoons yogurt dressing (see page 181)

Cook the potatoes in boiling, salted water for 20 minutes until tender. Drain well, cut into 1.2-cm (½-inch) cubes and place in a mixing bowl with the onion. Pour over the French dressing and leave to cool.

Cut the tomatoes into 1.2-cm (½-inch) cubes and add to the potatoe mixture together with the nasturtium leaves and yogurt dressing. Mix once again, carefully, and turn into a shallow serving dish.

Salade cauchoise

Serves 4

This famous French salad from the Caux area of Normandy is a mixture of celery, potatoes and smoked ham in a creamy dressing. This could be adapted to make a light luncheon dish by increasing the quantity of ham and serving with a green salad and brown bread.

500g (1lb) waxy new potatoes, scrubbed
2 tablespoons French dressing (see page 175)
3 sticks celery, thinly sliced
2 tablespoons chopped parsley
50g (2oz) smoked ham
180ml (6 fl oz) yogurt dressing (see page 181)

Cook the potatoes in boiling, salted water until just tender. Drain, cut into chip shapes and place in a bowl with the French dressing. Toss to coat and leave to cool.

Add the celery, parsley and ham and pour over the yogurt dressing. Toss thoroughly but carefully, then transfer to a shallow serving dish.

Barleycorn salad

Serves 4 to 6

Pot barley is preferable to the pearl variety, as it has a better flavour and more fibre. If you forget to soak the barley overnight, an extra 20 minutes' cooking will do as well.

125g (4oz) pot parley, soaked overnight
salt
5 tablespoons shoyu dressing (see page 180)
1 large red pepper, cored, seeded and chopped
75g (3oz) raisins
2 sticks celery, diced
2 tablespoons chopped parsley
4 spring onions, sliced
198-g (7-oz) can sweetcorn, drained
2 tablespoons sunflower seeds, roasted

Drain the barley, cover with cold water, add salt and bring to the boil. Cover and cook for 30 minutes until tender.

Drain well and mix with the shoyu dressing while still warm, then leave to cool.

Add the remaining ingredients and toss well, then transfer to a shallow serving dish.

Barley and spinach salad

Serves 4 to 6

An unusual salad which is hearty enough to serve as a light lunch, with crusty bread. Use pot barley instead of the pearl variety, as it is still in the husk and therefore full of fibre.

75g (3oz) pot barley, washed
2 tablespoons French dressing (see page 175)
500g (1lb) spinach, washed
150ml (¼ pint) yogurt
salt and pepper
1 clove garlic, crushed
4 spring onions, chopped

Cook the barley in boiling, salted water for 50 minutes until softened. Drain thoroughly, then place in a bowl with the French dressing. Toss thoroughly and leave to cool.

Cook the spinach in a large pan, with just the water clinging to the leaves, for 5 minutes. Drain thoroughly and chop finely.

Season the yogurt with salt and pepper to taste, then stir in the garlic and spring onions.

Add the spinach to the barley and mix together, then pour over the yogurt mixture and toss thoroughly.

Tabbouleh

Serves 4

This is a favourite dish in the Middle East, and is one of the quickest and easiest of salads to prepare. The basic ingredient is bulgur, or burghul, wheat, which is a cracked and partially cooked wheat, ready to eat after soaking and needing no further cooking.

75g (3oz) bulgur wheat
4 spring onions, chopped
4 tablespoons chopped mint
4 tablespoons chopped parsley
2 tablespoons lemon juice
4 tablespoons olive oil
salt and freshly ground black pepper

Soak the wheat in cold water for 1 hour, then drain through muslin and squeeze dry.

Place in a mixing bowl with the remaining ingredients, adding seasoning to taste. Mix thoroughly, then turn into a shallow serving dish.

Bazargan

Serves 4

A delicious recipe of Claudia Roden's which I first tasted while working on BBC Television's programme 'A Taste of Health'. It is really a winter version of Tabbouleh (see page 97), using nuts and tomato purée instead of fresh herbs.

250g (8oz) bulgur wheat
3 tablespoons olive oil
1 onion, finely chopped
4 tablespoons tomato purée
few sprigs fresh mint, chopped or 1 tablespoon dried mint
1 teaspoon ground cumin
1 teaspoon ground coriander
½ teaspoon ground allspice
125g (4oz) walnuts, coarsely chopped
juice of 1 lemon

Soak the bulgur wheat in cold water for about 15 minutes. Drain it well, squeezing out as much of the water as possible.

Heat 1 tablespoon of the oil in a pan and fry the onion until softened. Mix all the ingredients together in a bowl, and leave for about 1 hour for the bulgur to absorb the flavours and become plump and tender.

Transfer to a shallow bowl to serve.

Wholewheat and hazelnut salad

Serves 4 to 6

The wholewheat grain, or berry, used in this salad is readily available from natural food shops. But be warned – though very tasty and very good for you, it is also very chewy.

The first time I ate this salad, at a friend's house, my usual enthusiasm resulted in my absence from the conversation for about five minutes.

250g (8oz) wholewheat, soaked overnight and drained
salt
6 tablespoons shoyu dressing (see page 180)
1 red pepper, cored, seeded and chopped
1 green pepper, cored, seeded and chopped
50g (2oz) hazelnuts, chopped and browned
50g (2oz) currants
2 tablespoons chopped parsley

Cook the wheat in boiling, salted water, covered, for 1 to 1½ hours. Drain well and rinse, then place in a bowl with the dressing. Mix together, then leave until cool.

Add the remaining ingredients, toss thoroughly and transfer to a serving dish.

Persian rice salad

Serves 4

An unusual rice salad, using fresh dates and spices, which would make any cold meat plate more interesting but is particularly good with cold pork.

125g (4oz) brown rice
1 tablespoon sunflower oil
50g (2oz) cashew nuts
½ teaspoon ground cinnamon
1 teaspoon ground cumin
1 red pepper, seeded and chopped
175g (6oz) fresh dates, stoned and chopped
6 spring onions, sliced diagonally
4 tablespoons ginger dressing (see page 181)

Place the rice in a pan of boiling, salted water and simmer for 30 to 40 minutes, until tender. Rinse well and drain thoroughly.

Heat the oil in a small pan, add the cashew nuts and fry until beginning to turn golden. Add the cinnamon and cumin and fry for a further few seconds.

Place the rice in a bowl and add the cashew nuts and spiced oil from the pan. Mix in the red pepper, dates and onions.

Pour over the dressing and toss thoroughly.

Brown rice and raisin salad

Serves 6 to 8

A very filling salad which makes a useful and economical buffet dish. It would also be very good as an accompaniment to a barbecue, especially for young people.

175g (6oz) brown rice
6 tablespoons shoyu dressing (see page 180)
50g (2oz) raisins
50g (2oz) peanut kernels, toasted
1 red pepper, seeded and chopped
125g (4oz) frozen peas, cooked
1 small onion, finely chopped
2 sticks celery, chopped

Place the rice in a pan of boiling, salted water and simmer for 30 to 40 minutes, until tender. Rinse well and drain thoroughly.

Turn the rice into a bowl while still warm. Mix with the dressing and allow to cool.

Add the remaining ingredients and toss thoroughly before serving in a shallow dish.

Wild rice salad

Serves 4

Technically this is not a rice at all but comes from a wild, aquatic grass, native to North America. As it has to be gathered by hand, from a boat, it is extremely expensive. For this reason I have used a brown and wild rice mixture.

This salad is especially suitable to serve with game and poultry dishes.

125g (4oz) brown rice and wild rice, mixed and washed
4 tablespoons French dressing, but using walnut oil (see pages 13, 175)
50g (2oz) walnuts, chopped
1 dessert pear, quartered, cored and chopped
6 spring onions, sliced diagonally
3 sticks celery, sliced diagonally

Cook the rice in boiling, salted water for 30 minutes, until tender. Drain, rinse well and drain again.

Place in a bowl and add the dressing while the rice is still warm. When it is cool, add the remaining ingredients and mix together thoroughly.

Turn on to a shallow serving dish.

Pasta pesto

Serves 4

I have chosen to use the spiral-shaped *fusilli* pasta for this recipe, but any shape pasta will do. *Pesto* is an Italian sauce, made from basil, pine nuts and Parmesan cheese, which I have adapted to make a dressing for this salad.

125g (4oz) fusilli
4 tomatoes, skinned and chopped
1 small onion, sliced
50g (2oz) black olives, halved and stoned
6 tablespoons pesto *vinaigrette (see page 185)*

Cook the pasta in plenty of boiling, salted water for 10 to 12 minutes until *al dente*. Drain and rinse well, then drain again thoroughly.

Place the pasta in a bowl with the remaining ingredients and toss together well.

Pasta with courgettes and tomato

Serves 4 to 6

For this salad use very small, young courgettes and slice them very thinly to allow the flavour of the dressing to be absorbed.

125g (4oz) wholewheat elbow pasta
175g (6oz) courgettes, thinly sliced
6 tablespoons French dressing (see page 175)
6 small tomatoes, sliced
50g (2oz) black olives, halved and stoned
½ teaspoon dried oregano

Cook the pasta in plenty of boiling, salted water for 12 to 15 minutes until *al dente*. Drain and rinse well, then drain again thoroughly and leave to cool.

Place the courgettes in a bowl, pour over the dressing and leave to marinate for about 30 minutes.

Add the pasta, tomatoes, olives and oregano, toss thoroughly and transfer to a salad bowl.

Cucumber salad

Serves 4

The addition of chive flowers makes this a very pretty salad as well as giving it flavour.

This refreshing salad is suitable to serve with cold salmon or other fish. It is also ideal with any curried dish.

½ cucumber, sliced
salt
300ml (½ pint) yogurt
freshly ground black pepper
3 chive flowers, separated into florets

Slice the cucumber thinly, place in a colander, sprinkle with salt and leave for 30 minutes. Rinse well and pat dry with kitchen paper.

Mix the yogurt with black pepper to taste, then pour over the cucumber and mix together thoroughly.

Turn into a serving bowl and sprinkle with the chive flowers.

Cucumber and carrot salad

Serves 4

A pretty salad, the thin green and orange slices giving good contrast. The slightly sharp dressing goes well with the nutty flavour of roasted sesame seeds.

¼ cucumber
2 carrots, very thinly sliced
1 tablespoon shoyu*
2 tablespoons cider vinegar
freshly ground black pepper
1 tablespoon sesame seeds, roasted

Slice the cucumber thinly, then cut in half to form semicircles. Place in a bowl with the carrot and pour over the shoyu and vinegar. Add pepper to taste, sprinkle over the sesame seeds and toss well until coated.

Marinated courgettes

Serves 4

This is a salad to make when the first young, tender courgettes appear in the shops. Choose carefully and slice thinly to obtain the best results. It is a light, fresh salad, also good as a first course.

250g (8oz) courgettes, thinly sliced
2 carrots, scrubbed and thinly sliced
6 tablespoons French dressing (see page 175)
1 tablespoon chopped marjoram
1 tablespoon chopped parsley
50g (2oz) black olives, halved and stoned
3 tablespoons pine nuts, toasted

Place the courgettes and carrots together in a bowl with the dressing, and toss together thoroughly. Leave for several hours, turning occasionally.

Add the herbs, olives and pine nuts, mix together well again and then transfer to a serving dish.

Mushroom and red pepper salad

Serves 4

Marinating has many advantages over cooking. Preparation is quick and easy, and it not only gently softens the vegetables without making them mushy but also retains all the nutritional value and, at the same time, imparts a pleasant piquancy.

125g (4oz) courgettes, thinly sliced
125g (4oz) button mushrooms, sliced
4 tablespoons French dressing (see page 175)
1 red pepper, seeded and sliced
125g (4oz) beanshoots

Place the courgettes in a bowl with the mushrooms and pour over the French dressing. Toss well until coated, then leave to marinate for 1 hour.

Add the red pepper and beanshoots, toss again thoroughly and serve in a shallow dish.

Marinated mushrooms

Serves 4

I have been surprised to discover that many people are not aware that the pretty flowers of the chive plant are just as edible as the leaves.

They have a strong, distinctive flavour and impart a piquancy, as well as decoration, to this attractive dish.

250g (8oz) button mushrooms
6 tablespoons garlic dressing (see page 175)
2 tablespoons chopped parsley
3 chive flowers

Cut the mushrooms into quarters and place in a bowl with the dressing. Mix together well and leave to marinate for about 1 hour.

Add the parsley, mix well and transfer to a shallow serving dish.

Pull individual florets from the chive flowers, and sprinkle them over the mushrooms.

Cauliflower and bacon salad

Serves 4

Cauliflower can be a bit bland, so I've spiced this one up with peppery nasturtium leaves, a mustard dressing, and crisply fried bacon sprinkled over the top.

1 medium cauliflower, divided into florets
2 slices bacon, rinds removed, chopped
2 hard-boiled eggs, roughly chopped
6 nasturtium leaves, finely shredded
6 tablespoons mustard dressing (see page 179)

Cook the cauliflower in boiling, salted water for 2 minutes, drain and leave to cool. Fry the bacon in its own fat until crisp.

Place the cauliflower in a bowl with the chopped egg and nasturtium leaves. Pour over the dressing and toss thoroughly.

Turn into a serving bowl and sprinkle with the bacon.

Cauliflower and beanshoot salad

Serves 6

I think the flavour of cauliflower is enhanced if it is blanched and cooled before being added to a salad. This is a personal choice – some people prefer the crunchy texture of raw cauliflower. Either will be suitable for this tasty and satisfying salad.

500g (1lb) cauliflower, divided into florets
1 red pepper, halved and seeded
125g (4oz) beanshoots
2 tablespoons chopped chives
6 tablespoons mustard dressing (see page 179)
2 tablespoons sesame seeds, roasted

Cook the cauliflower in boiling, salted water for 2 minutes, drain and leave to cool.

Cut the red pepper into very thin slices, then place it in a bowl with the cauliflower, beanshoots and chives.

Pour over the dressing, toss thoroughly and transfer to a shallow serving dish. Sprinkle with the sesame seeds.

Broad bean and cauliflower salad

Serves 4 to 6

Choose young broad beans; if they are too large you will need to remove the skins, because they can be rather tough. This, of course, removes valuable fibre too.

250g (8oz) shelled broad beans
350g (12oz) cauliflower, broken into florets
6 spring onions, sliced diagonally
250ml (8fl oz) avocado dressing (see page 183)
1 tablespoon chopped parsley

Cook the beans in boiling, salted water for 10 minutes, drain, rinse under running cold water, then drain again and allow to cool.

Cook the cauliflower florets in boiling, salted water for 3 minutes, drain and cool.

Place the beans and cauliflower in a bowl with the spring onions and pour over the dressing. Mix well to coat, then transfer to a shallow serving dish and sprinkle with the parsley.

French bean vinaigrette

Serves 4

A simple but delicious first course which is equally good made with young, thin leeks when they are in season.

250g (8oz) French beans, topped and tailed
salt
75g (3oz) lean bacon, rind removed, chopped
1 hard-boiled egg, finely chopped
4 tablespoons vinaigrette dressing (see page 175)

Place the beans in a pan of boiling, salted water and simmer gently for 8 minutes. Drain well and place in a bowl.

Fry the bacon in its own fat until crisp, then add to the beans.

Add the egg to the dressing, pour over the beans and toss thoroughly. Transfer to a serving dish.

Tomato and bean vinaigrette

Serves 6

An attractive variation of this salad is to arrange all the vegetables in rows on a flat serving plate, and sprinkle with the dressing.

This, of course, takes more time, but is worth the effort for the visual effect on a special occasion.

500g (1lb) tomatoes, skinned
250g (8oz) French beans, topped and tailed
½ cucumber
1 red pepper, seeded and cut into strips
4 tablespoons vinaigrette dressing (see page 175)

Cut each tomato into 8 or 10 thin wedges, depending on its size, and place in a bowl.

Blanch the beans in boiling, salted water for 3 minutes, then drain and rinse under cold water to preserve the colour.

Cut the cucumber into fingers measuring about 5mm by 5cm (¼ inch by 2 inches) and place in the bowl with the beans and red pepper.

Pour over the dressing, toss thoroughly and transfer to shallow serving dish.

Rainbow bean salad

Serves 8

This bean salad is always popular, and very useful when you have to feed a lot of people at a buffet party or family get-together.

125g (4oz) red kidney beans, soaked overnight
125g (4oz) butter beans, soaked overnight
125g (4oz) shelled broad beans
125g (4oz) French beans, cut into 2.5-cm (1-inch) lengths
1 red pepper, seeded and chopped
2 sticks celery, sliced diagonally
125g (4oz) frozen sweetcorn, cooked
salt and freshly ground black pepper

Drain the kidney and butter beans, place in separate pans and cover with cold water. Bring to the boil and simmer the kidney beans for 1¼ to 1½ hours, the butter beans for 45 minutes, adding salt towards the end of cooking time. Drain the beans and place in a bowl.

Cook the broad beans and French beans in boiling, salted water for 7 to 8 minutes, until just tender. Drain well and add to the bowl. Pour over the dressing while the beans are still warm, and mix together well.

Cool, then stir in the pepper, celery, sweetcorn and seasoning to taste. Turn into a shallow serving dish.

Pinto bean and courgette salad

Serves 4

Don't let the idea of raw courgettes put you off this one. Thinly sliced and marinated in French dressing they are delicious, and this may well become one of your favourite salads!

175g (6oz) courgettes, thinly sliced
3 tablespoons French dressing (see page 175)
175g (6oz) cooked pinto beans
25g (1oz) black olives, halved and stoned
3 small tomatoes, each cut into 12 wedges

Place the courgettes in a bowl, toss in the dressing and leave to marinate for 2 hours.

Add the beans, olives and tomatoes and toss thoroughly. Serve in a shallow dish.

Sprouted mung salad

Serves 4

If you sprout mung beans at home you can, of course, use them at varying stages. This salad is nicest when the sprouts are still quite short, at which stage they have a more nutty flavour. You can buy these ready sprouted in some natural food shops. For instructions on sprouting beans at home see page 26.

175g (6oz) sprouted mung beans
2 tomatoes, chopped
2 sticks celery, chopped
2 tablespoons chopped parsley
6 spring onions, sliced finely
4 tablespoons shoyu dressing (see page 180)

Place the sprouted beans in a bowl with the tomatoes, celery, parsley and spring onions.

Pour over the dressing and toss thoroughly until well coated.

Black-eye bean salad

Serves 6

Savory goes particularly well with beans, but if you cannot get hold of any, use 2 tablespoons of chopped parsley instead.

250g (8oz) black-eye beans, soaked overnight
salt
6 tablespoons tomato dressing (see page 183)
4 tomatoes, skinned and chopped
3 sticks celery, thinly sliced
125g (4oz) garden peas, cooked
1 tablespoon chopped fresh savory

Drain the beans, place in a pan, cover with cold water and bring to the boil. Cover and cook for 30 minutes until soft, adding salt towards the end of cooking.

Drain well and mix with the dressing while still warm, then leave to cool.

Add the remaining ingredients, toss well to coat completely, then transfer to a serving dish.

Spicy chick pea salad

Serves 6 to 8

If you need to make this salad in a hurry, or simply want to take a short cut, it is equally successful if made with tinned chick peas and this, obviously, saves a great deal of time in preparation.

250g (8oz) chick peas, soaked overnight
salt
4 tablespoons tomato dressing (see page 183)
1 tablespoon tomato purée
1 teaspoon ground cumin
1 green pepper, seeded and chopped
1 small onion, finely chopped
4 tomatoes, skinned and chopped
1 tablespoon chopped fresh coriander

Drain the chick peas, place in a pan and cover with cold water. Bring to the boil and simmer for 1½ to 2 hours, until softened, adding a little salt towards the end of the cooking time. Drain well and turn into a bowl.

Mix the tomato dressing with the tomato purée and cumin, and pour over the chick peas while they are still warm. Toss well and leave to cool.

Add the remaining ingredients, mix thoroughly, then turn into a shallow serving dish.

Lentil and walnut salad

Serves 6 to 8

The lentil is the only pulse that does not require soaking before cooking. The green lentil retains its shape when cooked, which makes it ideal for salads.

250g (8oz) green lentils
salt
6 tablespoons garlic dressing (see page 175)
2 sticks celery, chopped
500g (1lb) tomatoes, skinned and chopped
50g (2oz) walnuts, roughly chopped
2 tablespoons chopped parsley
2 tablespoons chopped chives
freshly ground black pepper

Place the lentils in a pan of boiling, salted water and simmer for 35 to 40 minutes, until softened. Drain well, place in a bowl and pour over the dressing while still warm. Mix well and then leave to cool.

Add the remaining ingredients with enough black pepper to taste. Mix together well, then transfer to a shallow serving dish.

Radish and arame salad

Serves 4

A most attractive salad to look at and equally tasty to eat. Seaweed is all too after ignored in our diet, which is a great pity as it is an extremely valuable source of vitamins and minerals.

15g (½oz) arame*
426ml (¾ pint) water
¼ cucumber
1 bunch radishes, thinly sliced
2 tablespoons chopped chives
½ teaspoon Dijon mustard
1 tablespoon cider vinegar
1 tablespoon apple juice
½ teaspoon clear honey
freshly ground black pepper

Soak the arame in the water for 5 minutes, then bring to the boil, cover and simmer for 20 minutes. Remove the lid and cook for a further 10 minutes until the liquid has evaporated, then allow to cool.

Cut the cucumber into sticks measuring 3mm by 5cm (⅛ inch by 2 inches), then place in a bowl with the arame, radishes and chives. Mix the mustard, vinegar, apple juice, honey and pepper to taste together, then pour over the salad and toss thoroughly. Transfer to a shallow serving dish.

Arame and carrot salad

Serves 4

Arame is a seaweed, harvested in Japan, which has a mild, sweet flavour. It is rich in many valuable minerals and is therefore ideal to serve in the winter months when salad ingredients are in short supply.

> 15g (½oz) arame,* washed
> 426ml (¾ pint) water
> 1 tablespoon cider vinegar
> 1 teaspoon shoyu*
> freshly ground black pepper
> 3 spring onions, sliced diagonally
> 125g (4oz) carrots, grated
> 1 tablespoon sesame seeds
> 1 tablespoon chopped parsley
> radish roses to garnish (see page 16)

Soak the arame in water for 5 minutes, then bring to the boil, cover and simmer for 20 minutes. Remove the lid and cook for a further 10 minutes, until the liquid has evaporated, then allow to cool.

Mix the arame with the vinegar, shoyu and black pepper to taste and leave to marinate for 30 minutes. Add the spring onions, carrots and sesame seeds.

Toss thoroughly and turn into a shallow serving dish. Sprinkle with the parsley and garnish with the radishes.

Celeriac and sorrel salad

Serves 4

Celeriac is in season during the winter months, which makes it a valuable salad ingredient when little else of unusual interest is available. It has the texture of potato and the flavour of celery.

Celeriac makes an intriguing salad when mixed with sorrel and egg and coated in a creamy yogurt dressing.

500g (1lb) celeriac, peeled
salt
2 tablespoons French dressing (see page 175)
2 hard-boiled eggs
few sorrel leaves, finely shredded
6 tablespoons yogurt dressing (see page 181)

Cut the celeriac into chunks and cook in boiling, salted water for about 15 minutes until tender. Drain well, then place in a bowl with the French dressing, mix thoroughly and leave to cool.

Cut the eggs into chunks and add to the celeriac with the sorrel. Pour over the yogurt dressing, mix well, then transfer to a serving dish.

Beetroot and cress salad

Serves 4

Raw beetroot has a sweet, earthy flavour which is enlivened by the orange dressing. Grate very finely (using a julienne blade on a food processor, if you have one) to give long, thin strands. This will ensure that the beetroot thoroughly absorbs the orange flavour of the dressing, which is the essence of this delicious salad.

350g (12oz) raw beetroot, peeled
3 tablespoons orange dressing (see page 177)
2 cartons mustard and cress, washed and drained

Grate the beetroot very finely, place in a bowl with the orange dressing and toss gently. Leave to marinate for at least 15 minutes.

Immediately before serving add the cress to the bowl and mix again, gently.

Beetroot and fennel salad

Serves 4

This is a salad to please the eye as much as the palate. The beetroot creates a wonderful colour when mixed with the semtana – a deep fuchsia pink – and the delicate fronds of fennel add the perfect finishing touch to this delightful salad.

250g (8oz) cooked beetroot
2 dill cucumbers
2 tablespoons chopped fennel
120ml (4 fl oz) smetana*
1 teaspoon lemon juice
salt and freshly ground black pepper

Cut the beetroot and dill cucumbers into 1-cm (½-inch) dice and place in a mixing bowl.

Mix all but a little of the fennel with the smetana, lemon juice and seasoning to taste. Pour over the beetroot and mix thoroughly.

Turn into a shallow serving dish and sprinkle with the remaining fennel.

Parsnip with curry vinaigrette

Serves 4

Parsnips are not generally considered a salad vegetable, but they do make a very good salad when grated finely. The addition of curry powder and chopped nuts creates a tangy, crunchy salad with a very individual flavour.

This salad stimulates conversation at the table, as few of my guests recognize the vegetable and many think it to be some exotic introduction from the East.

500g (1lb) parsnips, peeled
½ teaspoon curry powder
2 tablespoons chopped parsley
5 tablespoons vinaigrette dressing (see page 175)
25g (1oz) hazelnuts, chopped and browned

Grate the parsnips finely, preferably with a julienne blade in a food processor, if you have one. Mix the curry powder and parsley with the dressing and pour over the parsnips in a bowl.

Toss well to coat completely and leave to marinate for about 30 minutes.

Transfer to a serving dish and sprinkle the nuts over the top.

Kohlrabi vinaigrette

Serves 4

Kohlrabi is delicious eaten raw with a French dressing. The name is derived from the German words *kohl*, meaning cabbage, and *rübe*, meaning swede, thus accounting for the cabbage-like leaves on top and the fleshy stem which is the part eaten, tasting very similar to turnip.

500g (1lb) kohlrabi,* peeled
4 tablespoons French dressing (see page 175)
1 tablespoon chopped parsley

Grate the kohlrabi, using a julienne blade on a food processor. Pour the dressing over and toss thoroughly, using two forks.

Transfer to a shallow serving dish and sprinkle with parsley.

Okra salad

Serves 4

This delicate and rather pretty vegetable from tropical Africa is also known as 'Ladies' Fingers'.

Be careful not to overcook, or it will split and lose its attractive appearance.

250g (8oz) okra*
2 tablespoons oil
1 onion, sliced
2 cloves garlic, crushed
1 teaspoon cumin
1 teaspoon turmeric
4 tomatoes, skinned and chopped
1 tablespoon chopped fresh coriander

Cut away the conical cap of the okra, without exposing the seeds.

Heat the oil in a pan and fry the onion until softened. Add the garlic, cumin and turmeric and fry for 1 minute, then add the tomatoes and okra. Cover and simmer gently for 20 minutes, until the okra is soft. Allow to cool, then transfer to a serving dish and sprinkle with the coriander.

Jerusalem artichoke salad

Serves 4 to 6

Jerusalem artichokes are better scrubbed than peeled, as they retain more flavour and food value. This also relieves you of an extremely tedious chore, as some come in weird and knobbly shapes and sizes. Be careful not to overcook them, as they will become mushy.

500g (1lb) Jerusalem artichokes, scrubbed
salt
4 tablespoons French dressing (see page 175)
2 sticks celery, thinly sliced
2 tablespoons chopped parsley

Cut the artichokes into small, even-sized pieces and cook in a pan of boiling, salted water for 10 to 15 minutes until just tender – they should still remain a little resistant.

Drain well, reserving the water for a soup.

Place in a bowl with the dressing while still warm, and mix together carefully. When cool add the celery and parsley, toss again and transfer to a serving dish.

Artichoke and broad bean salad

Serves 4 to 6

Jerusalem artichokes have an intriguing flavour which blends particularly well with broad beans.

As for Jerusalem Artichoke Salad, leave them unpeeled, thus saving flavour and fibre, time and temper!

500g (1lb) Jerusalem artichokes, scrubbed
250g (8oz) shelled broad beans
2 tablespoons sunflower seeds, toasted
2 tablespoons chopped parsley
6 tablespoons French dressing (see page 175)

Cut the artichokes into small even-sized pieces and place in a pan of boiling, salted water. Bring to the boil, cover and simmer gently for 10 to 15 minutes, until they are tender; do not boil them too hard or too long or they will break up and become mushy. Drain well and leave to cool.

Cook the beans in boiling, salted water for 10 minutes, drain, rinse under running cold water, then drain again and allow to cool.

Place the artichokes in a bowl with the beans, add the remaining ingredients and mix together with the dressing. Transfer to a shallow serving dish.

Sweetcorn salad

Serves 4 to 6

One of my favourite salads, which we often have as a light but satisfying supper dish, with crusty brown bread to mop up the dressing. The spring greens must be finely sliced – they need a lot of chewing!

125g (4oz) spring greens, washed
4 tablespoons shoyu dressing (see page 180)
250g (8oz) sweetcorn
3 sticks celery, finely sliced
4 spring onions, chopped

Roll the spring greens into a tight bundle and shred very finely. Place in a mixing bowl with the dressing, toss thoroughly and leave to marinate for about one hour, tossing once or twice.

Cook the sweetcorn in boiling, salted water for 4 to 5 minutes, then drain well and cool. Add to the greens with the celery and spring onions, toss once again thoroughly and serve.

Orange and onion salad

Serves 4

An unusual salad, very refreshing, and attractive too. It could be the perfect answer when you are looking for a salad to complement a rich main course.

3 large oranges
1 small purple onion, thinly sliced
25g (1oz) black olives, halved and stoned
4 tablespoons lemon dressing (see page 176)
1 tablespoon chopped parsley

Peel the oranges and slice across into rounds. Place in a bowl with the onion rings and olives, pour over the dressing and toss thoroughly.

Arrange on a serving dish and sprinkle with the parsley.

Onion with yogurt and coriander

Serves 4

A simple and very refreshing salad, ideal to serve with spicy dishes. I use it as an accompaniment to lentil croquettes or nut rissoles.

1 teaspoon tomato purée
1 teaspoon ground cumin
150ml (¼ pint) natural yogurt
2 onions, finely sliced
1 tablespoon chopped fresh coriander

Mix the tomato purée and cumin together in a small bowl, then gradually add the yogurt until blended.

Mix with the onions and coriander and transfer to a serving dish.

Mangetout and mint vinaigrette

Serves 4

The mint brings out all the flavour of these delicious crisp and tasty peas.

Just top and tail, pulling off any strings, and if they are rather large, cut in half diagonally. The pods should be quite flat, the tiny peas only just showing their shape.

125g (4oz) mangetout peas
2 heads chicory
2 carrots, scraped
2 tablespoons chopped mint
3 tablespoons lemon vinaigrette (see page 176)

Top and tail the mangetouts and blanch in boiling, salted water for about 2 minutes. Drain well and leave to cool.
Cut the chicory into 1.2-cm (½-inch) diagonal slices, separate the leaves and add to the mangetouts. Slice the carrots very thinly on a mandoline or in a food processor, and add to the bowl with the mint. Pour over the dressing, toss thoroughly and transfer to a shallow serving dish.

Radish and sesame vinaigrette

Serves 4

Quite a fiery salad, but a very pretty one. Good to clear the palate after a rich main course.

1 bunch radishes, topped and tailed
175g (6oz) white radish (Daikon),* peeled
3 tablespoons vinaigrette dressing (see page 175)
1 bunch watercress, washed
1 tablespoon sesame seeds, toasted

Slice the red and white radishes finely, using a mandoline if you have one. Pour over the dressing and mix thoroughly.

Arrange the watercress sprigs on a flat serving plate and spoon the radishes over the top, leaving a border of watercress round the edge. Sprinkle with the sesame seeds.

Pickled radish salad

Serves 4

The Japanese use mild, white radish, or Daikon, in many recipes and it is very popular when pickled. The pickling liquid can be used again but it is also useful to add to soups.

> *175g (6oz) Daikon radish,* peeled*
> *1 tablespoon shoyu*
> *1 teaspoon finely chopped ginger*
> *2 tablespoons water*

Slice the radish thinly and place in a bowl. Mix the shoyu, ginger and water together and pour over.

Cover and leave overnight in the refrigerator. Serve with cold meats as a pickle.

Cooked vegetable salad

Serves 4 to 6

This type of cooked salad is frequently found in Indonesia. The vegetables you use can be varied according to what is available, but be careful not to overcook them or they will lose their crispness.

The coconut dressing can be made more, or less, spicy as you wish by varying the amount of chilli powder used.

125g (4oz) Dutch cabbage, roughly chopped
125g (4oz) French beans, cut in half
2 carrots, scraped and thinly sliced
250g (8oz) broccoli, broken into florets
125g (4oz) beanshoots
6 tablespoons coconut cream dressing (see page 186)
1 tablespoon sesame seeds

Blanch the cabbage, beans, carrots and broccoli in boiling, salted water for 3 minutes. Drain well and place in a salad bowl with the beanshoots.

Pour over the coconut dressing and toss well, but carefully, to coat thoroughly.

Sprinkle with the sesame seeds and serve warm or cold.

Waldorf salad

Serves 6

A well-known salad from America named after the famous Waldorf Hotel, the salad having been created for its opening.

Excellent to serve with cold pork or ham, it is also frequently eaten as a light lunch.

3 russet dessert apples
150ml (¼ pint) yogurt mayonnaise (see page 178)
4 sticks celery, chopped
25g (1oz) walnut pieces
2 tablespoons chopped chives

Quarter and core the apples, chop roughly and place in a bowl with the mayonnaise. Add the celery and walnuts, and mix together until all the vegetables are well coated.

Turn on to a shallow serving dish and sprinkle with the chives.

Fay's crunch

Serves 8

A delicious salad, given to me by a friend. She particularly likes
to serve it with a barbecue, but it is so appetizing that I would
suggest you serve it whenever you can get hold of some fresh
dates.

Don't chop the vegetables too finely, or the result will be
mushy.

2 Cox's Orange Pippin apples, quartered and cored
120ml (4fl oz) mayonnaise (see page 177)
4 tablespoons yogurt
250g (8oz) fresh dates
1 red pepper, halved, seeded and diced
50g (2oz) hazelnuts, chopped and browned
4 sticks celery, chopped
50g (2oz) raisins
2 tablespoons chopped parsley

Chop the apples roughly, place in a bowl with the mayonnaise
and yogurt and toss well to coat, so that they will not discolour.

Cut the dates in half lengthways and remove the stone. Cut in
half again and add to the bowl with the remaining ingredients.
Toss thoroughly and turn into a salad bowl.

Minted melon and grape salad

Serves 4

Impressive and truly delicious, but very speedily and easily
made, this is the perfect choice for a first course when the rest of
the meal you have planned takes time to prepare.

So long as you have all the ingredients to hand it can be made
in a matter of moments.

750g (1½lb) watermelon
125g (4oz) beanshoots
125g (4oz) black grapes, halved and seeded
2 tablespoons chopped mint
3 tablespoons lemon dressing (see page 176)

Cut the melon into slices, cut out the flesh, discard the seeds, and cut into cubes. Place in a bowl with the beanshoots, grapes and mint. Pour over the dressing and toss well until coated. Turn into a shallow serving dish.

Light Meals and Snacks

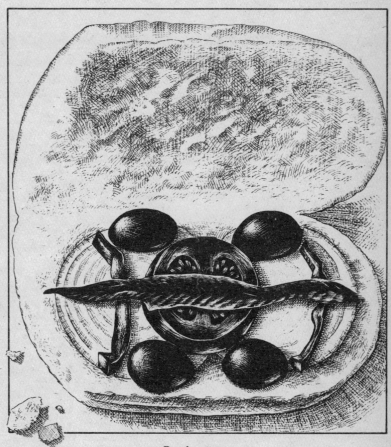

Pan bagna

Duck liver salad

Serves 4

An unusual and interesting *Salade Tiède* which will require last-minute finishing to ensure that the duck liver is served warm.

1 small radicchio
2 large heads chicory
1 bunch watercress, washed and broken into sprigs
175g (6oz) back bacon, rind removed
3 tablespoons hazelnut oil
175g (6oz) duck livers, cut into strips
1 clove garlic, chopped
2 tablespoons raspberry wine vinegar
salt and freshly ground black pepper

Break the radicchio into manageable pieces and place in a salad bowl. Slice the chicory diagonally, separate the layers and place in the bowl with the watercress.

Cut the bacon into ½-cm (¼-inch) wide strips and place in a frying pan with the oil. Fry for 2 minutes, then add the duck liver and garlic and fry lightly, turning to seal the outsides, but still leaving the inside of the duck liver pink.

Turn on to the salad ingredients. Add the vinegar to the pan and stir round over the heat to dissolve all the juices.

Pour over the salad, adding seasoning to taste, then toss thoroughly and serve immediately.

Gammon and spinach salad

Serves 4

Gammon and spinach is an old favourite, but in this recipe the roles have been reversed so that spinach is the more important ingredient. I'm sure those of you with prolific spinach beds will find this an invaluable addition to your salad repertoire.

750g (1½lb) spinach, washed
1 clove garlic, crushed
¼ teaspoon grated nutmeg
150ml (¼ pint) yogurt dressing (see page 181)
4 spring onions, finely chopped
125g (4oz) smoked ham, diced

Cook the spinach in a little salted water for about 5 minutes. Drain thoroughly, chop roughly, place in a bowl and leave to cool.

Add the garlic and nutmeg to the dressing and mix well, then pour over the spinach, adding the onions and ham.

Mix together thoroughly and transfer to a shallow serving dish.

Smoked mackerel and apple salad

Serves 4

Smoked mackerel and horseradish are natural partners, but the partnership is made even happier by the addition of apple and celery in this very palatable salad.

2 Cox's Orange Pippin apples, quartered and cored
2 tablespoons French dressing (see page 175)
2 sticks celery, thinly sliced
3 tablespoons chopped parsley
2 smoked mackerel, skinned and boned
150ml (¼ pint) horseradish dressing (see page 187)

Slice the apples into a bowl and toss in the dressing to prevent them browning. Add the celery and parsley, toss again and set aside.

Flake the fish into fairly large pieces and arrange on one side of a serving dish. Coat with the horseradish dressing to cover completely, then spoon the salad on to the other half of the dish.

Gravlax

Serves 4

Highly popular in its native Scandinavia, and also highly popular with me, Gravlax is particularly good when accompanied by Fennel and Alfalfa Salad (see page 78) and rye bread.

2 tablespoons fine sea salt
2 tablespoons clear honey
·1 teaspoon black pepper
2 tablespoons chopped dill
750-g (1½-lb) tail piece of salmon, filleted

DILL DRESSING
2 tablespoons German mustard
1 tablespoon clear honey
1 tablespoon white wine vinegar
4 tablespoons olive oil
4 tablespoons smetana*
2 tablespoons chopped dill

Mix together the salt, honey, pepper and dill and sprinkle half the mixture over the base of a shallow dish. Lay the salmon on top and sprinkle with the remaining dill mixture. Cover and leave to marinate for 2 to 3 days in the refrigerator, turning the salmon, carefully, each day.

To make the dill dressing, beat the mustard, honey and vinegar together. Gradually add the oil, beating well between each addition, then stir in the smetana and most of the dill.

Remove the skin from the salmon and cut the fish into 3-mm (⅛-inch) wide strips, across the grain. Arrange on a flat serving dish, pour the dill dressing down the centre, and sprinkle with the remaining dill.

Scandinavian herring salad

Serves 4

Fennel is one of the most popular herbs in Scandinavia. In this recipe its slightly aniseed taste blends perfectly with the pickled cucumber and herring.

300g (10oz) rollmop herrings
3 pickled dill cucumbers
250g (8oz) cooked potato, diced
125g (4oz) cooked beetroot, diced
3 hard-boiled eggs, chopped
2 tablespoons chopped fennel
150ml (¼ pint) yogurt dressing (see page 178)

Unroll the rollmops and cut into diagonal slices 1cm (½ inch) wide. Slice the dill cucumbers thinly and place in a bowl with the herring, potato, beetroot, eggs and most of the fennel.

Pour over the dressing and mix together gently until coated.

Transfer to a shallow serving dish and sprinkle with the remaining fennel.

Butter bean and tuna salad

Serves 4

This hearty salad, with an Italian tang to it, would be good at any time, but being quick and easy to put together it makes a super *ad hoc* summer lunch.

198-g (7-oz) can tuna fish, drained
4 spring onions, chopped
4 tomatoes, skinned
400-g (14-oz) can butter beans, drained
2 sticks celery, sliced
25g (1oz) black olives, halved and stoned
1 tablespoon chopped marjoram
4 tablespoons French dressing (see page 175)

Flake the tuna fish into large pieces and place in a salad bowl with the spring onions.

Cut each tomato into 8 wedges and add to the bowl with the beans, celery, olives and marjoram.

Pour over the dressing and toss together until thoroughly coated.

Transfer to a dish and serve with crusty wholewheat garlic bread.

Haricot bean salad

Serves 4

A pretty salad of contrasting colours, very quickly made with canned haricot beans.

400-g (14-oz) can haricot beans, drained
4 tablespoons French dressing (see page 175)
3 tablespoons chopped parsley
50g (2oz) black olives, halved and stoned
2 hard-boiled eggs
3 tomatoes

Place the beans in a bowl with the dressing, parsley and olives. Cut each egg and tomato into 8 wedges and add to the bowl. Carefully mix to coat with the dressing and serve in a shallow dish.

Rice and bean salad

Serves 6 to 8

Brown rice and beans are both staple foods, providing a lot of nourishment. Served and eaten together they balance each other to provide the protein equivalent, ounce for ounce, of a rump steak.

125g (4oz) brown rice
salt
4 tablespoons shoyu dressing (see page 00)
1 red pepper, cored, seeded and diced
2 sticks celery, chopped
198-g (7-oz) can sweetcorn, drained
397-g (14-oz) can red kidney beans, drained
4 spring onions, chopped
2 tablespoons chopped parsley

Cook the rice in boiling, salted water for 30 to 35 minutes, until tender. Rinse well, drain and place in a bowl with the dressing. Toss thoroughly and leave to cool.

Add the remaining ingredients and mix well together. Transfer to a shallow dish and serve with crusty brown bread.

Flageolet and ham salad

Serves 4

Served with granary bread, this salad makes a really excellent light lunch.

The butter beans and ham are very satisfying, and the mustard dressing and gherkin add a delightful flavour.

175g (6oz) butter beans, soaked overnight
salt
4 tablespoons mustard dressing (see page 179)
175g (6oz) smoked ham, cubed
2 tablespoons chopped parsley
1 small onion, finely chopped
25g (1oz) gherkins, sliced

Drain the beans, place in a pan and cover with cold water. Bring to the boil and simmer gently for 45 minutes, until tender, adding a little salt towards the end of the cooking time. Drain well, place in a bowl with the dressing and mix together.

When cool, add the ham, parsley, onion and gherkins and mix together until everything is well coated.

Transfer to a shallow serving dish.

Potato and prawn salad

Serves 4

A very good salad to include in a cold buffet, especially to accompany salmon. Served with a green salad, and with the addition of extra prawns, it would also make a substantial supper dish.

500g (1lb) waxy potatoes, scrubbed
salt
125g (4oz) shelled prawns
2 tablespoons chopped dill
120ml (4fl oz) tomato cream dressing (see page 184)

Cook the potatoes in boiling, salted water until tender. Drain well, chop roughly and leave to cool.

Place the potatoes in a bowl with the prawns and dill. Pour over the dressing and mix thoroughly, then transfer to a shallow serving dish.

Potato niçoise

Serves 4

An unusual potato salad which I particularly like with cold turkey or chicken.

3 tablespoons olive oil
1 onion, chopped
500g (1lb) potatoes, cut into 1-cm (½-inch) cubes
1 red pepper, seeded and sliced
1 green pepper, seeded and sliced
2 cloves garlic, finely chopped
4 tomatoes, skinned and chopped
2 tablespoons water
salt and freshly ground black pepper
50g (2oz) black olives, halved and stoned
1 tablespoon chopped parsley

Heat the oil in a heavy-based pan and fry the onion, potatoes, peppers and garlic for about 10 minutes, stirring frequently.

Add the tomatoes, water and seasoning to taste, cover and cook for a further 30 minutes, stirring occasionally. Stir in the olives and allow to cool.

Transfer to a shallow serving dish, sprinkle with the parsley and serve with cold meats.

Potato and bacon salad

Serves 4

New potatoes served in their skins are always popular and are delicious when combined with crisply cooked bacon. This nourishing and satisfying salad would be ideal for a quick lunch or supper dish.

500g (1lb) baby new potatoes, scrubbed
1 tablespoon French dressing (see page 175)
4 rashers lean bacon, rind removed
2 hard-boiled eggs
6 tablespoons smetana dressing (see page 186)

Cook the potatoes in boiling, salted water for 15 minutes until tender. Drain well, cut in half if large and place in a mixing bowl with the French dressing. Toss thoroughly and leave to cool.

Cut the bacon into 1-cm (½-inch) strips and fry in a non-stick frying pan until crisp.

Cut each egg into 8 wedges and add to the potatoes with the bacon. Toss in the smetana dressing and serve in a shallow dish.

Spring green and bacon salad

Serves 4 to 6

The combined flavours of the greens with the shoyu, bacon and sweetcorn blend together wonderfully well. The greens need to be shredded very finely, as they are definitely chewy, but they do soften slightly after marinating in the dressing.

250g (8oz) spring greens
120ml (4 fl oz) shoyu dressing (see page 180)
125g (4oz) lean bacon
olive oil for frying
198-g (7-oz) can sweetcorn, drained
6 spring onions, chopped

Shred the spring greens very finely, discarding the very thick parts of the stalks. Place in a bowl, pour over the dressing, toss thoroughly and leave to marinate for 1 hour, tossing occasionally.

Cut the rind from the bacon, chop and fry in a little olive oil for 2 minutes, stirring constantly.

Add to the bowl with the sweetcorn and spring onions.

Jutta's (pronounced 'yoota') potato salad

Serves 4

A delicious salad which I first tasted at a picnic lunch by the river, during Henley Royal Regatta week. It was served by a German friend, after whom I've named it.

500g (1lb) waxy potatoes, scrubbed
salt
2 tablespoons French dressing (see page 175)
3 pickled dill cucumbers, thinly sliced
3 hard-boiled eggs, roughly chopped
1 small onion, finely chopped
6 tablespoons smetana dressing (see page 186)
fronds of fennel to garnish

Cook the potatoes in their skins in boiling, salted water for about 20 minutes until tender. Drain well, cut into 1.5-cm (¾-inch) cubes and place in a mixing bowl. Pour the French dressing over them while they are still warm so that they absorb it completely, mix well and leave to cool.

Add the dill cucumbers, eggs and onions, pour over the smetana dressing, and mix together carefully.

Turn into a shallow serving dish and garnish with fronds of fennel.

Pan bagna

Serves 4

A delicious Provençal salad sandwich, eaten in so many cafés in that area at any time of day. Perfect for a beach picnic.

1 large French loaf
6 tablespoons garlic dressing (see page 175)
1 small onion, thinly sliced
3 tomatoes, sliced
small green pepper, seeded and cut into rings
49-g (1¾-oz) can anchovies, drained
25g (1oz) black olives, halved and stoned

Split the French loaf along one side, without cutting right through the crust. Open it out so that it lies flat. Sprinkle the dressing evenly over the bread.

Place the onion, tomato and pepper slices on one side of the loaf. Arrange the anchovies and olives over the top and close the two halves, pressing firmly together.

Wrap in foil and place on a baking sheet, lay another on top and put a 907-g (2-lb) weight on top to press together for 30 minutes. This will allow the dressing and salad to mingle into the bread, and also make it easier to eat.

Cut the loaf into four diagonal slices.

Salade niçoise

Serves 4

The ingredients for this salad depend on the season and what is available. It is nearly always served as a first course in France, but it has become a firm favourite with my family as a summer lunch. Serve with plenty of garlic bread.

1 small crisp lettuce, washed
500g (1lb) tomatoes
198-g (7-oz) can tuna fish, drained
½ cucumber, sliced
1 small onion, thinly sliced
250g (8-oz) French beans, cooked
3 hard-boiled eggs, quartered
50g (2oz) black olives, halved and stoned
1 red pepper, deseeded and roughly chopped
6 tablespoons garlic dressing

Arrange the lettuce leaves in a salad bowl. Cut the tomatoes into wedges, flake the tuna fish and add to the bowl.

Add all the remaining ingredients and toss in the dressing before serving.

Italian tuna salad

Serves 4 to 6

A light and satisfying meal, ideal as a snack before or after an evening out.

75g (3oz) penne pasta
4 tomatoes, skinned
6 spring onions, sliced diagonally
2 sticks celery, thinly sliced
198-g (7-oz) can tuna fish, drained
1 avocado pear, halved and stoned
300ml (½ pint) smetana dressing (see page 186)

Cook the pasta in plenty of boiling, salted water for 10 to 12 minutes until *al dente*. Drain and rinse well, then drain again thoroughly.

Cut the tomatoes into wedges, then place in a bowl with the onions, celery and pasta.

Flake the tuna into large pieces, peel the avocado and cut into large chunks, then add to the salad with the dressing.

Toss carefully, then transfer to a shallow serving dish.

Curried pasta salad

Serves 4 to 6

A successful blending of continental with oriental. The pasta and chicken are deliciously flavoured by the pineapple and curry, and with the celery to add a touch of crunch it really is a delight.

75g (3oz) pasta shells
350g (12oz) cooked chicken
2 sticks celery, sliced diagonally
200-g (7-oz) can pineapple slices, drained
300ml (½ pint) curry mayonnaise (see page 178)
1 tablespoon chopped parsley

Cook the pasta in plenty of boiling, salted water for 10 to 12 minutes, until *al dente*. Drain and rinse well, then drain again thoroughly and place in a bowl.

Cut the chicken into chunks, then add to the bowl with the celery. Cut the pineapple into 1.25-cm (½-inch) pieces and add to the bowl with the mayonnaise.

Mix carefully, then transfer to a shallow serving dish and sprinkle with the parsley.

Cauliflower and Stilton salad

Serves 4

The combination of cauliflower and Stilton is particularly pleasant, but any other blue cheese may be substituted if you prefer.

1 cauliflower, broken into florets
salt
125g (4oz) Stilton cheese, cut into cubes
50g (2oz) hazelnuts, roughly chopped and browned
1 bunch watercress
6 tablespoons yogurt dressing (see page 181)

Cook the cauliflower in boiling, salted water for 2 minutes. Drain, rinse in cold water, drain again and leave to cool.

Place in a bowl with the cheese and nuts. Wash the watercress well, shake dry, then break into sprigs and add to the bowl with the dressing; toss together until well coated. Transfer to a shallow serving dish.

Summer salad

Serves 4

Another salad to make use of the juicy red home-grown tomatoes available in late summer.

Superb with basil, but also good with chives if basil is unobtainable.

350g (12oz) cottage cheese
500g (1lb) tomatoes, skinned and chopped
¼ cucumber, diced
1 tablespoon chopped basil
salt and freshly ground black pepper
4 lettuce leaves

Place the cheese in a mixing bowl with the tomatoes, cucumber and basil. Season with the salt and pepper to taste, and mix together thoroughly.

Place the lettuce leaves on individual plates and spoon some salad on to each one.

Fattoush

Serves 4

This traditional Lebanese salad is one of those extremely useful dishes that can be modified to make use of available ingredients. Properly, it should be made with pitta bread but I use wholewheat instead. Like most traditional peasant dishes it is both versatile and very tasty.

2 thick slices stale wholewheat bread, cut into cubes
6 tablespoons French dressing (see page 175)
125g (4oz) feta cheese
3 tomatoes, chopped
¼ cucumber, cut into cubes
15g (1oz) black olives, halved and stoned
1 green pepper, seeded and chopped
40-g (1¾-oz) can anchovies, drained
2 tablespoons chopped parsley

Place the bread in a bowl, pour over the dressing and mix well. Add the cheese, tomatoes, cucumber, olives and pepper.

Cut the anchovies into 2.5-cm (1-inch) pieces and add to the bowl, with the parsley.

Mix together carefully then transfer to a serving dish.

Greek salad

Serves 4

This salad always reminds me of lovely, sun-drenched holidays in Greece, and I make it on our return home to try to prolong happy memories.

Fortunately it is now possible to purchase all the ingredients of an authentic Greek salad, including the essential feta cheese, in most supermarkets here.

Remember that feta cheese is inclined to be salty, so go gently with the seasoning.

½ cucumber
1 small onion, thinly sliced into rings
1 green pepper, cored, seeded and chopped
500g (1lb) tomatoes
3 tablespoons olive oil
1 tablespoon cider vinegar
1 tablespoon chopped fresh basil
1 tablespoon chopped marjoram
salt and freshly ground black pepper
250g (8oz) feta cheese, cut into cubes
125g (4oz) black olives, stoned

Cut the cucumber into large dice and place in a bowl with the onion and green pepper. Cut each tomato into 8 wedges and add to the bowl with the oil, vinegar, herbs, salt and pepper to taste. Toss thoroughly and turn into a salad bowl.

Sprinkle the cheese over the top, decorate with the olives and serve with lots of crusty bread to mop up the juices.

Tomato and mozzarella salad

Serves 4

A delicious salad to make when your greenhouse is bulging
with tomatoes. Choose really ripe ones – their sweet juiciness
blends perfectly with the mild, soft mozzarella.

This also makes a perfect first course.

500g (1lb) Marmande tomatoes
2 Italian mozzarella cheeses
3 tablespoons French dressing (see page 175)
3 tablespoons chopped parsley

Slice the tomatoes thinly and arrange overlapping slices on
individual plates. Slice the mozzarella into rounds and arrange
overlapping slices on top of the tomatoes.

Pour a little dressing over each one, the sprinkle parsley
generously over the top.

Cheese and apple salad

Serves 4

I make this simple salad for my lunch during the autumn, when
the russet apples in the garden are ripe.

Very quick, easy and nourishing – serve with crusty granary
bread.

4 dessert apples, quartered and cored
4 tablespoons French dressing (see page 175)
175g (6oz) Cheddar cheese, cut into cubes
2 tablespoons chopped parsley
25g (1oz) hazelnuts, chopped and browned
lettuce leaves to serve

Chop the apples and place in a bowl with the dressing. Toss
thoroughly to coat the apple, so that it will not turn brown. Add

the cheese, parsley and hazelnuts, and mix together.

Arrange the lettuce leaves on individual plates and spoon some salad on top.

Gado gado

Serves 4 to 6

This is an unusual salad, consisting of raw and cooked vegetables, which is sufficiently satisfying to serve as a light meal.

A traditional Indonesian dish, it is served with a piquant peanut dressing.

175g (6oz) waxy potatoes, cut into chunks
salt
250g (8oz) cauliflower, broken into florets
2 large carrots, scraped and sliced
175g (6oz) French beans, topped, tailed and cut in half
125g (4oz) spring greens, roughly chopped
125g (4oz) beanshoots
¼ cucumber, sliced
2 hard-boiled eggs, sliced

SPICY PEANUT DRESSING
1 tablespoon sunflower oil
1 small onion, chopped
1 clove garlic, crushed
1 teaspoon ground cumin
1 teaspoon ground coriander
½ teaspoon chilli powder
3 tablespoons crunchy peanut butter
150ml (¼ pint) water
1 teaspoon shoyu*
1 teaspoon lemon juice

Cook the potatoes in boiling, salted water until tender, then drain and leave to cool. Cook the cauliflower, carrots, beans and spring greens in boiling, salted water for about 3 minutes, then rinse in cold water and drain well.

To make the peanut dressing, heat the oil in a pan and fry the onion until softened. Add the garlic and spices and fry for a further 2 minutes, stirring.

Mix in the peanut butter then blend in the water, bring to the boil, stirring, then cover and cook for 5 minutes. Stir in the shoyu and lemon juice, and thin with a little more water if desired. Allow to cool.

Arrange the cooked vegetables on a serving platter to make an attractive design. Sprinkle the beanshoots over the top and garnish with the cucumber and egg slices. Pour over the dressing, or serve in a separate bowl.

Oriental tofu salad

Serves 4

Tofu is a soya bean curd, sold in slabs in Chinese supermarkets and health-food shops. Its bland flavour allows it to take on flavourings very easily; in this case the ginger dressing and sesame seeds impart a delicious taste. A further advantage of tofu is its very high protein content.

250g (8oz) firm tofu*
4 tablespoons ginger dressing (see page 181)
2 tablespoons sesame seeds, roasted
1 bunch watercress
125g (4oz) beanshoots

Cut the tofu into 1-cm (½-inch) cubes and place in a bowl with the dressing and sesame seeds. Toss carefully and leave to marinate for about 30 minutes.

Wash the watercress well, shake dry and divide into sprigs, then add to the bowl together with the beanshoots. Toss again thoroughly and transfer to a shallow serving dish.

Main Meals

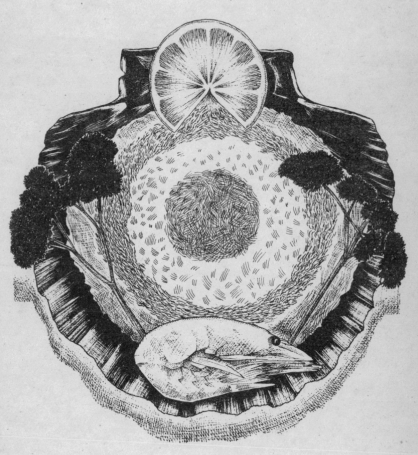

Crab salad

Turkey tonnato

Serves 4 to 6

If you are looking for something different to intrigue your guests, try this sliced turkey coated with a tuna fish mayonnaise. It makes an unusual and delicious lunch dish.

500g (1lb) turkey breast
1 carrot
1 stick celery
1 onion
bouquet garni
salt and freshly ground black pepper

SAUCE
4 tablespoons mayonnaise (see page 177)
75-g (3-oz) can tuna fish, drained
1 tablespoon anchovy essence
1 tablespoon lemon juice
freshly ground black pepper
150ml (¼ pint) yogurt

TO GARNISH
1 tablespoon capers
lemon slices

Place the turkey in a pan with the carrot, celery, onion, bouquet garni, seasoning and enough water to cover. Bring to the boil, cover and simmer gently for 30 minutes, until cooked. Allow to cool in the liquid.

To make the sauce, place the mayonnaise in the bowl of a food processor with the tuna fish, anchovy essence, lemon juice and pepper to taste. Blend until smooth, then gradually add to the yogurt to make a smooth sauce.

Slice the turkey breast thinly and arrange overlapping slices on a serving plate. Pour the sauce down the centre, sprinkle over the capers and garnish with lemon slices.

Turkey with cranberry vinaigrette

Serves 4

A very attractive salad, best served on individual plates. The sweet cranberry vinaigrette is a superb combination with the slightly bitter salad ingredients.

Complete the meal with wild rice salad.

500g (1lb) turkey breast, cooked
4 tablespoons walnut oil
2 tablespoons red wine vinegar
1 teaspoon Dijon mustard
1 tablespoon cranberry sauce
salt and freshly ground black pepper

SALAD
1 bunch watercress, washed and drained
½ small curly endive
few radicchio leaves
2 heads chicory
50g (1oz) walnuts, roughly chopped

Slice the turkey diagonally across the length of the breast, and arrange overlapping slices on one side of 4 individual plates.

Place the oil, vinegar, mustard, cranberry sauce and seasoning to taste in the bowl of a food processor, and blend until smooth.

Divide the watercress into sprigs, break the endive and radicchio into pieces, and place in a bowl. Cut the chicory into diagonal slices and add to the bowl. Pour over half the cranberry vinaigrette, toss thoroughly and arrange on the other side of the plates. Sprinkle the walnuts over the salad. Pour the remaining dressing over the turkey slices.

Magret de Canard

Serves 4

A superb main-course salad using just boneless breats of duck. Be sure to cook the duck until the skin is crisp and most of the fat has run out.

4 duck breasts (about 150g (5oz) each)
3 large heads chicory, sliced diagonally
2 oranges, peeled and cut into segments
few leaves radicchio, torn into pieces
4 tablespoons orange dressing (see page 177)
1 tablespoon chopped parsley
1 tablespoon sesame seeds, toasted

Place the duck breasts, skin side down, in a grill pan and cook under a moderate grill for 5 minutes. Turn the duck over and cook for a further 5 minutes, until the skin crisps and most of the fat has run out. Remove the duck from the grill and allow to cool until lukewarm.

Place all the salad ingredients together with half the dressing in a bowl and toss thoroughly until well coated with the dressing. Slice the duck thinly, arrange, overlapping slices down one side of 4 individual dinner plates, and spoon the remaining dressing over the duck. Arrange the salad on the other side of each plate.

Chicken and grape salad

Serves 4

A variation on the Coronation Chicken theme – chunks of cooked chicken mixed with grapes, celery and almonds in a mild curry mayonnaise.

You can use black or green grapes, but for this recipe I prefer black, for their colour. Do not cut the chicken too small, or the salad will lose its form.

This is an ideal salad for a summer buffet party, as it requires only a fork.

> 350g (12oz) cooked chicken
> 250g (8oz) black grapes, halved and seeded
> 2 sticks celery, thinly sliced
> 50g (2oz) split almonds, browned
> 240ml (8 fl oz) curry mayonnaise (see page 00)

Cut the chicken into fairly large pieces and place in a bowl with the grapes, celery and almonds. Pour over the mayonnaise and toss carefully to coat the chicken completely.

Transfer to a shallow plate and serve with a rice salad and a green salad.

Chicken and fruit vinaigrette

Serves 4 to 6

A light, but flavoursome and nourishing salad for a hot summer day. Ideal for those occasions when you know that a meal is needed, but your appetite lacks enthusiasm.

> 350g (12oz) cooked chicken breast
> 125g (4oz) black grapes, halved and seeded
> small Ogen melon, halved and seeded
> ¼ cucumber
> 6 tablespoons vinaigrette dressing (see page 175)
> 50g (2oz) split almonds, browned

Cut the chicken into fairly large chunks and place in a bowl with the grapes.

Remove the flesh from the melon with a melon scoop, and add to the chicken.

Cut the cucumber into 3-mm (⅛-inch) thick slices, then stack

them up and cut into quarters. Add to the bowl with the
dressing, and toss together well.

Turn into a shallow dish, sprinkle with the almonds, and
serve with a rice salad.

Oriental chicken salad

Serves 4

This is a super salad for a special occasion – easy to prepare,
impressive to serve and delicious to eat.

> *350g (12oz) cooked chicken breasts*
> *1 red pepper, seeded and thinly sliced*
> *250g (8oz) mangetouts*
> *225g (7oz) water chestnuts, drained*
> *25g (1oz) split almonds, browned*
> *6 tablespoons sesame dressing (see page 180)*

Cut the chicken into strips about 5mm (¼ inch) wide and place
in a bowl with the red pepper.

Top and tail the mangetouts, removing any strings, cut in half
diagonally if large, and blanch in boiling water for 3 minutes.
Drain and rinse under cold water to help preserve the colour.

Slice the water chestnuts thinly and add to the chicken with
the mangetouts and almonds. Pour over the dressing and mix
well.

Turn into a shallow dish and serve with crusty bread.

Mediterranean chicken salad

Serves 4

The holiday may be long gone, but the memory can be evoked by a glass of crisp, white wine and Mediterranean Chicken Salad.

Serve for lunch in the garden on a warm and sunny summer's day to preserve the illusion.

350g (12oz) cooked chicken breasts
125g (4oz) black olives, halved and stoned
8 small tomatoes, skinned
1 green pepper, seeded and thinly sliced
6 tablespoons garlic dressing (see page 175)
3 tablespoons chopped parsley

Cut the chicken into quite large pieces and place in a bowl with the olives.

Cut each tomato into 8 wedges and add to the bowl with the remaining ingredients. Toss thoroughly and leave to marinate for about 1 hour.

Turn on to a shallow dish and serve with potato salad.

Bœuf niçoise

Serves 6

Definitely a salad for the special occasion. The tender, succulent beef is easily managed with a fork, making this an excellent choice for a celebration buffet.

1.5-kg (3-lb) fillet of beef
3 tablespoons corn oil

RATATOUILLE
1 small aubergine
salt
4 tablespoons oil
1 onion, sliced
1 red pepper, cored, seeded and sliced
250g (8oz) courgettes, sliced
2 cloves garlic, crushed
freshly ground black pepper
1 teaspoon chopped marjoram
4 tomatoes, skinned and sliced

Tie the fillet at 2.5-cm (1-inch) intervals to keep a good shape. Heat the oil in a roasting pan, then add the beef and baste well. Cook in a hot oven (220°C/425°F/Gas Mark 7) for 40 to 45 minutes, basting occasionally. Cook 10 minutes longer if you prefer beef well cooked. Remove from the tin, allow to cool, then chill.

Make the ratatouille as described on page 69 and leave to cool. Remove the string from the beef and cut into thin slices with a very sharp knife. Arrange overlapping slices on a serving dish in a semicircle, and place the ratatouille in the remaining space.

Beef julienne salad

Serves 4

I use very little red meat, so when I do I like to make something a bit special. This salad is one I reserve for summer dinner parties, or small celebrations.

It is quite easy to make, but do be careful not to overcook the meat.

300g (10oz) button mushrooms
3 tablespoons French dressing (see page 175)
2 175-g (6-oz) fillet steaks
oil for brushing
6 spring onions
150ml (¼ pint) horseradish dressing (see page 187)
4 spring onion tassels (see page 17)

Slice the mushrooms and place in a bowl with the French dressing; leave for 30 minutes to marinate.

Brush the steaks with a little oil and place under a hot grill for 2 to 3 minutes on each side, depending on how rare you like it.

Allow the steaks to cool, then cut into strips measuring 3.5cm by 5mm (1½ inches by ¼ inch) and add to the mushrooms.

Cut the spring onions lengthways into fine strips, then into 3.5-cm (1½-inch) lengths. Add to the bowl and mix all the ingredients together.

Turn on to a flat serving dish, spoon the horseradish dressing down the centre and garnish with the spring onion tassels.

Crab salad

Serves 4

I recommend fresh crabs for this salad as frozen crab meat, while quick and easy, does not have such a good flavour. When buying the crabs, bear in mind that the female crab is usually smaller and has smaller claws than the male, so will contain less white meat. You can, of course, arrange the crab meat directly on a plate, but I think it looks much prettier arranged on scallop shells, which can usually be obtained from the fishmonger.

This is a delightful summer lunch, served with a crisp green salad and tomato cream dressing (see page 184) or plain mayonnaise.

2 375-g (12-oz) crabs
salt and freshly ground pepper
75g (3oz) wholewheat breadcrumbs
2 teaspoons lemon juice
milk to mix
4 scallop shells
1 hard-boiled egg
1 tablespoon finely chopped parsley
4 whole prawns
1 lemon, cut into wedges

Clean the crabs with a damp cloth and remove the claws and legs. Break the claws with nutcrackers or a hammer, remove the white meat with a skewer and place in a bowl. Remove the shells from the crabs and discard the stomach sac from behind the eyes. Discard the 'dead men's fingers' from the body and cut the body into quarters to facilitate the removal of the white meat. Add to the bowl and season to taste.

Scrape out all the brown meat from inside the shells and place in a bowl. Mix in the breadcrumbs and seasoning, lemon juice to taste and enough milk to make a soft consistency.

Spoon the brown meat into the base of each scallop shell, and surround with the whitemeat. Finely chop the egg white and sprinkle a little where the brown and white flesh meet. Sieve the egg yolk and arrange next to the egg white, then arrange the parsley next to the egg yolk. Garnish each with a prawn and place on a serving plate. Serve with lemon wedges.

Shellfish mayonnaise

Serves 4

A delicate dish, good enough to deserve your best friends and your best white wine. Serve with plenty of thinly sliced brown bread.

250g (8oz) peeled prawns
250g (8oz) cooked cod, flaked
4 tomatoes, skinned, seeded and shredded
1 avocado pear, halved and stoned
4 tablespoons mayonnaise (see page 177)
4 tablespoons yogurt
2 tablespoons chopped fennel
4 whole prawns to garnish

Place the prawns, cod and tomatoes in a mixing bowl. Skin the avocado, cut into chunks and add to the bowl.

Mix the mayonnaise, yogurt and fennel together, pour over the salad and mix carefully.

Turn on to a shallow dish, garnish with the prawns and serve with a rice salad.

Seafood rice salad

Serves 4

A fresh-tasting summer salad. The varieties of fish you use can be changed but it is essential always to choose a fish with firm white flesh.

125g (4oz) scallops, cleaned
250g (8oz) monkfish, cubed
250g (8oz) prawns, shelled
125g (4oz) cooked brown rice
½ cucumber, diced
4 tablespoons chopped chives
2 tablespoons chopped dill
120ml (4floz) lemon dressing (see page 176)

Place the scallops in a pan, cover with water and bring to the boil. Simmer gently for 2 minutes, then leave to cool. Drain, and cut each scallop across into 3 discs.

Poach the monkfish in the same way (but this will take about 6 minutes), then leave to cool.

Place all the fish in a bowl with the rice, cucumber, herbs and dressing, the mix together carefully until all are well coated.

Leave for about 1 hour before serving, so that the flavour of the herbs and lemon dressing permeates the rice and fish.

Turn on to a shallow dish and serve with a green salad.

Pasta and shellfish salad

Serves 4 to 6

Any type of pasta will do, but choose a pretty shape such as this spiral pasta or shells. To add a bit of character to this salad I always reserve a few mussels in their shells for a garnish. After cooking, pull away one of the shells from each of the reserved mussels and leave the fish, shell attached, in the other half.

125g (4oz) fusilli pasta
125g (4oz) button mushrooms
6 tablespoons French dressing (see page 175)
125g (4oz) peeled prawns
125g (4oz) cooked mussels, cooled
4 tomatoes, peeled and cut into wedges
2 tablespoons chopped parsley

Cook the pasta in plenty of boiling, salted water for 10 to 12 minutes until *al dente*. Drain and rinse well, then drain thoroughly.

Quarter the mushrooms and place in a large bowl with the dressing. Mix together and leave to marinate for 15 minutes.

Add the pasta, prawns, mussels, tomatoes and parsley, toss together well then transfer to a serving dish.

Stuffed eggs niçoise

Makes 16

In addition to being a very pleasant first course, this is an excellent dish to serve as part of a selection at a buffet meal.

8 hard-boiled eggs
50g (2oz) black olives, halved and stoned
75-g (3-oz) can tuna fish, drained
75g (3oz) curd cheese
4 tablespoons smetana*
2 teaspoons anchovy essence
1 tablespoon capers, chopped
shredded lettuce to garnish
4 tomatoes, quartered

Cut the eggs in half lengthways, remove the yolks and rub through a sieve.

Reserve 8 olive halves and chop the rest finely.

Mash the tuna fish with a fork, then mix with the cheese, smetana, anchovy essence, chopped olives, capers and sieved egg yolks.

Spoon the filling into the centre of each egg white, and shape into a mound. Garnish with the reserved olive halves.

Arrange the eggs on a bed of shredded lettuce, and put a tomato quarter between each egg.

Fruit Salads

Pineapple and strawberry salad

Currant kissel

Serves 4 to 6

A rich red fruit salad made from blackcurrants and redcurrants, flavoured with orange, and made potent with port.
Delicious served with whipped cream or yogurt.

500g (1lb) mixed black- and redcurrants
4 tablespoons clear honey
120ml (4fl oz) orange juice
2 teaspoons arrowroot
2 tablespoons water
3 tablespoons port

Place the currants in a pan with the honey and orange juice. Bring to the boil and simmer gently for 10 minutes, until softened.
Strain, reserving the syrup, and place the currants in a bowl.
Return the syrup to the pan and bring to the boil. Mix the arrowroot with a little water and stir into the boiling syrup.
Cook, stirring continuously, until thickened and clear.
Pour over the fruit, with the port, and leave to cool.

Raspberry and blackcurrant sundae

Serves 4

Use tall wine glasses for this sundae, so that you can more easily see the striped effect of the red fruit and creamy smetana.
I use smetana instead of cream as it has a far lower fat content and tastes wonderful with the slightly sharp, rich flavour of the fruit.

150ml (¼ pint) orange juice
2 tablespoons clear honey
250g (8oz) blackcurrants
2 teaspoons arrowroot
4 tablespoons port
250g (8oz) raspberries
300ml (½ pint) smetana*

Place the orange juice, honey and blackcurrants in a pan. Bring them to the boil, cover and simmer gently for 10 minutes until they are soft.

Strain the fruit, place in a bowl and return the syrup to the pan. Blend the arrowroot with a little cold water and add to the syrup. Bring to the boil, stirring, and cook until the syrup thickens and is clear. Pour over the currants, add the port and all but 4 of the raspberries, and leave to cool.

Spoon half the fruit mixture into 4 wine glasses, then spoon half the smetana into each glass. Cover with the remaining fruit mixture and top with the remaining smetana. Decorate with the reserved raspberries.

Pineapple and strawberry salad

Serves 4 to 6

One of those combinations of fruits that complement each other perfectly, and with the addition of orange-flower water and kirsch, the fruits take on an intriguing scented flavour.

This salad looks wonderful served in the pineapple shell, but of course tastes just as delicious served in a bowl, if you prefer.

1 large pineapple
250g (8oz) strawberries, halved
3 tablespoons orange-flower water
2 tablespoons kirsch

Cut the pineapple in half lengthways, cut out the flesh with a grapefruit knife, discard the central core and cut into cubes. Reserve the shells.

Place the cubes in a bowl with the strawberries, orange-flower water and kirsch. Spoon the juices over the fruit and leave to soak for about 2 hours in the refrigerator.

Arrange the shells on a serving plate and spoon the salad into the shells.

Strawberries in raspberry sauce

Serves 4

A simple dessert, but more interesting than plain strawberries. The Cointreau and raspberry sauce transforms a very normal summer dish into a sophisticated and luscious conclusion to a luncheon party.

> *350g (12oz) strawberries*
> *175g (6oz) raspberries*
> *2 tablespoons clear honey*
> *2 tablespoons Cointreau*

Divide the strawberries between 4 glass dishes. Sieve the raspberries, then stir in the honey and Cointreau.

Pour over the strawberries and chill until required. Serve with whipped cream or thick yogurt.

Fruit salad

Serves 6

There are any number of possible variations on this theme. I have chosen fruits which are easily available, blend well and taste good, and I like to use watermelon as a base because it looks so beautifully bright and appetizing.

> ½ watermelon
> 2 oranges, peeled and cut into segments
> 125g (4oz) strawberries, halved
> 2 bananas, sliced
> 125g (4oz) black grapes, halved and seeded
> 125g (4oz) green grapes, halved and seeded
> 4 tablespoons orange juice
> 2 tablespoons Grand Marnier

Cut the watermelon into wedges and cut out the flesh. Discard the seeds and cut the flesh into cubes. Place in a bowl with the rest of the fruit.

Mix the orange juice and liqueur together and pour over the fruit. Leave to macerate for about 1 hour, stirring occasionally.

Spoon the fruit into individual serving dishes and pour over the juice.

Yogurt fruit salad

Serves 4

One of the simplest and yet most delicious fruit salads I know. It takes only a few minutes to make and is always a great success.

> 300ml (½ pint) yogurt
> 2 teaspoons clear honey
> 2 tablespoons Grand Marnier
> 125g (4oz) strawberries
> 125g (4oz) raspberries

Mix the yogurt, honey and liqueur together until smooth. Slice the strawberries and add to the yogurt with the raspberries. Mix together gently and spoon into wine glasses.

Tropical fruit salad

Serves 6 to 8

A *mélange* of magical fruit flavours which blend together to form
a mouthwatering and memorable dessert, gorgeous at any time,
but perfect for a balmy summer evening.

1 pineapple
411-g (14½-oz) can guavas
2 bananas, sliced
2 oranges
lemon balm to decorate

Cut the pineapple into quarters lengthways, remove the skin
and cut the flesh into chunks, discarding the central core.
  Place the chunks in a bowl with the guavas and bananas.
  Remove the peel and pith from the oranges, divide them into
segments and add to the salad.
  Decorate with a sprig of lemon balm.

Kiwi in Cointreau

Serves 4

The kiwi, or Chinese gooseberry, is a native of China but is now
grown in many countries, principally New Zealand.
  When making this dish leave the fruits to macerate in the
juices for at least an hour, so that they absorb the flavour of the
Cointreau.

2 kiwi fruits, peeled and thinly sliced
125g (4oz) black grapes, halved and seeded
4 tablespoons apple juice
2 tablespoons Cointreau
1 Ogen melon, halved and seeded
lemon balm sprigs to decorate

Place the kiwi fruits in a bowl with the black grapes and pour over the apple juice and Cointreau.

Scoop the flesh from the melon halves with a melon baller, or cut into cubes, and add to the fruit.

Leave to soak for 1 hour in the refrigerator, stirring occasionally. Spoon the fruit into individual glass dishes, pour over the juice and decorate with sprigs of lemon balm.

Dried fruit salad

Serves 4

An ideal winter dessert when few fresh fruits are available. Excellent served with Greek yogurt or smetana.

125g (4oz) dried apricots
125g (4oz) pitted prunes
125g (4oz) dried figs
450ml (½ pint) orange juice
150ml (¼ pint) water
2 oranges, peeled and cut into segments
25g (1oz) flaked almonds, toasted

Place the dried fruits in a bowl with the orange juice and water, and leave to soak overnight.

Transfer to a saucepan, cover and simmer for 15 minutes, then leave to cool. Add the orange segments, turn into a glass bowl and sprinkle with the almonds.

Hunza apricot and orange salad

Serves 4

These delicious little apricots come from the Hunza valley in Northern India. They taste, and look, quite different from the usual dried apricots. They have the appearance of shrivelled brown balls, due to the fact that they have not been sprayed with sulphur dioxide to preserve their colour.

When cooked they swell into perfect tiny apricot shapes, and are so sweet that no sugar is needed.

They are easily obtainable from health-food shops.

175g (6oz) Hunza apricots
600ml (1 pint) water
3 oranges
25g (1oz) flaked almonds, toasted

Place the apricots in a pan with the water. Bring to the boil, cover and simmer very gently for 15 minutes. Leave to cool in the saucepan.

Peel the pith from the oranges and cut into segments, using a sharp knife. Mix with the apricots and turn into a glass bowl.

Chill in the refrigerator and sprinkle with the almonds just before serving.

Dressings

French dressing

Makes about 450ml (¾ pint)

Olive oil is a must for this dressing; it imparts a rich, fruity flavour, especially if you use that lovely green, virgin olive oil.

I make a large quantity at a time and store it in ꞁ wine bottle, ready for instant use.

350g (12 fl oz) olive oil
90ml (3 fl oz) cider vinegar
1 tablespoon Moutarde de Meaux
1 clove garlic, crushed
1 teaspoon clear honey
salt and freshly ground black pepper

Pour the oil into a measuring jug and make up 450ml (¾ pint) with the vinegar.

Add the remaining ingredients then, using a funnel, pour into a wine bottle. Put in the cork, firmly, give the mixture a good shake, and store.

VARIATION:

Garlic dressing

Add a further 3 cloves of crushed garlic to the above ingredients.

Vinaigrette dressing

Makes about 250ml (8 fl oz)

A vinaigrette dressing is basically a French dressing with added chopped herbs. My favourites are mint, parsley and chives, with a little thyme.

The lemon variation is much better with fruit-based salads.

150ml (5 fl oz) olive oil
3 tablespoons cider vinegar
1 clove garlic, crushed
1 teaspoon clear honey
2 tablespoons chopped mixed herbs

Put all the ingredients in a screw-top jar, adding salt and pepper to taste, and shake well before using.

VARIATIONS:

Lemon or lime vinaigrette

Use 3 tablespoons fresh lemon juice or lime juice in place of the cider vinegar.

Raspberry vinaigrette

Use 3 tablespoons raspberry wine vinegar in place of the cider vinegar.

Lemon dressing

Makes 120ml (4 fl oz)

A good dressing to use with any fruit-based savoury salad.

juice of 1 large lemon
2 tablespoons clear honey
2 tablespoons olive oil
salt and freshly ground black pepper

Put all the ingredients in a screw-top jar, adding salt and pepper to taste. Shake well to blend before serving.

Orange dressing

Finely grate the rind of 1 orange and blend with a little of the squeezed juice. Add the remaining ingredients with the rest of the orange juice and mix thoroughly.

Lime dressing

Substitute the juice of 1 lime for the lemon juice.

Mayonnaise

Makes 300ml (½ pint)

This is the basic method of making mayonnaise without a blender.

I find that mayonnaise made with olive oil alone is rather heavy, so I combine it with corn or sunflower oil.

2 egg yolks
pinch salt
freshly ground black pepper
½ tablespoon Dijon mustard
150ml (¼ pint) olive oil
150ml (¼ pint) corn oil
1 tablespoon wine vinegar

Beat the egg yolk and seasonings together in a bowl. Add the oil drop by drop, beatring vigorously. As it thickens add the remaining oil in a steady stream, beating constantly.

Stir in the vinegar and mix thoroughly.

Quick method

Use 1 whole egg instead of 2 yolks, place in the bowl of the food processor with the seasonings and the vinegar, and blend for a few seconds. Add the oils through the lid, slowly at first then in a steady stream as it thickens.

Yogurt mayonnaise

Makes 300ml (½ pint)

This recipe retains the delicious mayonnaise flavour, but has almost half the usual fat content.

150ml (¼ pint) mayonnaise
150ml (¼ pint) yogurt

Mix the mayonnaise and yogurt together until smooth.

Curry mayonnaise

Makes 240ml (8 fl oz)

I find that a jar of concentrated curry sauce is very useful for this mayonnaise. It keeps for months, and does not have the harsh flavour of uncooked spices.

1 teaspoon concentrated curry sauce
2 teaspoons tomato purée
2 teaspoons clear honey
2 tablespoons mayonnaise
150ml (¼ pint) smetana*

Mix the curry sauce, tomato purée and honey together, then mix into the mayonnaise.

Add the smetana gradually. Store in the refrigerator.

Mayonnaise niçoise

Makes 250ml (8 fl oz)

A delicious mayonnaise to serve with potato or egg dishes.

150ml (¼ pint) mayonnaise
1 tomato, peeled and chopped
1 clove garlic, crushed
1 tablespoon capers, drained
1 tablespoon tomato purée
1 tablespoon anchovy essence
freshly ground black pepper

Place all the ingredients together in the bowl of a food processor, and blend until smooth.

Mustard dressing

Makes 120ml (4 fl oz)

Good for any salads to which you want to add an extra tang.

4 tablespoons olive oil
1 tablespoon lemon juice
2 tablespoons apple juice
1 tablespoon Moutarde de Meaux
1 clove garlic, crushed
salt and freshly ground pepper

Place all the ingredients in a screw-top jar, adding salt and pepper to taste. Shake well to blend before serving.

Sesame dressing

Makes 120ml (4 fl oz)

A piquant dressing with a rich, creamy texture, which could well become a firm favourite.

2 tablespoons tahini (sesame paste)*
2 tablespoons rice vinegar
2 tablespoons medium sherry
2 tablespoons sesame oil
1 tablespoon shoyu*
1 clove garlic, crushed

Place the sesame paste in a bowl and gradually mix in the vinegar and sherry.

Add the oil, shoyu and garlic and mix together thoroughly.

Shoyu dressing

Makes 250ml (8 fl oz)

The best dressing to use with grain-based salads.

150ml (¼ pint) sunflower oil
3 tablespoons shoyu*
2 tablespoons lemon juice
2 cloves garlic, crushed
freshly ground black pepper

Put all the ingredients in a screw-top jar, adding pepper to taste, and shake well to blend.

VARIATION:

Ginger dressing

Add a 2.5-cm (1-inch) piece of peeled and very finely chopped root ginger to the above ingredients.

Yogurt dressing

Makes 150ml (¼ pint)

A good low-fat general-purpose dressing to use in place of mayonnaise.

150ml (¼ pint) yogurt
1 clove garlic
1 tablespoon lemon juice
1 teaspoon clear honey
salt and freshly ground black pepper

Place all the ingredients in a bowl, adding salt and pepper to taste, and mix thoroughly with a fork.

VARIATION:

Yogurt and basil dressing

Add 2 tablespoons chopped basil to the above ingredients, and serve with tomato salads.

Hazelnut dressing

Makes 120ml (4 fl oz)

A sweet, nutty dressing, ideal to serve with any cabbage or celery salad.

6 tablespoons apple juice
25g (1oz) hazelnuts, roasted
small clove garlic
salt and freshly ground black pepper
4 tablespoons Greek yogurt

Place the juice, nuts, garlic and seasoning to taste in a liquidizer or food processor, and blend until smooth.

Gradually add to the yogurt, and store in the refrigerator for up to 4 days.

Green herb dressing

Makes 250ml (8 fl oz)

A lovely fresh dressing that goes particularly well with cauliflower and broad beans.

15g (1/2oz) parsley
15g (1/2oz) mint
15g (1/2oz) chives
1 clove garlic, crushed
150ml (1/4 pint) yogurt
salt and freshly ground black pepper

Remove the stalks from the parsley and mint and place the leaves in a food processor with the remaining ingredients, adding seasoning to taste.

Blend for 1 to 2 minutes, until smooth, then store in the refrigerator.

Tomato dressing

Makes 175ml (6 fl oz)

Particularly good with beans and pulses, this is probably one of the least fattening dressings I know.

150ml (¼ pint) tomato juice
2 tablespoons lemon juice
1 tablespoon shoyu*
1 clove garlic, crushed
2 tablespoons chopped chives
1 teaspoon clear honey
salt and freshly ground black pepper

Place all the ingredients together in a screw-top jar and shake well before serving.

VARIATION:

Tomato and caper dressing

Add 1 tablespoon chopped capers to the above ingredients. Delicious with any egg-based salad.

Avocado dressing

Makes 450ml (¾ pint)

A good dressing to serve with tomato, prawns and many green cooked vegetables, such as broad beans or broccoli, and an excellent treatment for those soft avocados you can't really serve halved or sliced.

1 avocado pear, halved and stoned
170ml (6 fl oz) smetana*
2 tablespoons milk
2 teaspoons lemon juice
½ teaspoon Worcester sauce
1 teaspoon grated onion
salt and freshly ground pepper

Peel the avocado, cut into chunks and place in a food processor or blender, with the remaining ingredients. Blend to a purée, adding a little more milk if you require a thinner dressing.

Roquefort dressing

Makes 170ml (6 fl oz)

When you're feeling a bit extravagant, treat yourself to this elegant dressing. You'll find your salads take on a new dimension.

50g (2oz) Roquefort cheese
150ml (¼ pint) yogurt
2 tablespoons chopped chives
freshly ground black pepper

Mash the Roquefort with a fork, then gradually blend in the yogurt until smooth.
    Add the chives and black pepper to taste.

Tomato cream dressing

Makes 300ml (½ pint)

The smooth and creamy texture and delicious flavour of this dressing are the perfect complement to any fish salad. It would also add a gourmet touch to a salad of melon or avocado.

2 tomatoes, skinned, seeded and chopped
1 clove garlic, crushed
2 teaspoons tomato purée
1 teaspoon clear honey
120ml (4 fl oz) smetana*
salt and freshly ground pepper

Place all the ingredients in a liquidizer and blend until smooth.

Pesto vinaigrette

Makes 250ml (8 fl oz)

I make this delicious dressing whenever I have sufficient basil, and use it mostly with large Marmande tomatoes for a simple first course. It also blends well with potatoes and cold pasta salads.

4 tablespoons chopped basil
4 tablespoons chopped parsley
1 small clove garlic, crushed
15g (½oz) pine or cashew nuts
1 tablespoon Parmesan cheese
150ml (¼ pint) olive oil
3 tablespoons lemon juice
freshly ground black pepper

Place all the ingredients in the blender with black pepper to taste. Blend for about 1 minute, until smooth.

If this amount is more than you need to use, the surplus can be stored in an airtight container in the refrigerator for several weeks.

 notation# THE SALAD BOOK

notation## Coconut cream dressing

notation### Makes 250ml (8 fl oz)

A spicy dressing to serve with cooked vegetable salads.

notation50g (2oz) creamed coconut, chopped
4 tablespoons boiling water
2 cloves garlic, crushed
pinch chilli powder
2 tablespoons lemon juice
4 tablespoons yogurt

Blend the coconut with the boiling water until a smooth cream is formed. Add the remaining ingredients and mix together thoroughly.

notation## Smetana dressing

notation### Makes 175ml (6 fl oz)

A useful creamy dressing.

notation150ml (¼ pint) smetana*
3 teaspoons lemon juice
salt and freshly ground black pepper

Mix all the ingredients together in a bowl and store in the refrigerator for up to 4 days.

Horseradish dressing

A pungent creamy dressing, rather like a thin mayonnaise in consistency. It is particularly good with beef and smoked fish; also with beetroot and potato salads.

Add 3 tablespoons horseradish relish to the above ingredients and leave for 30 minutes before using.

List of Herb Specialists

Hollington Nurseries
Woolton Hill
Newbury
Berks
Tel Highclere 253908

A delightful nursery set in a walled garden.
Open all summer
Closed on Sundays between October and March

Iden Croft Herb Farm
Frittenden Road
Staplehurst
Kent TN12 0DH
Tel 0580 891432

Open 7 days a week in summer
Closed on Sundays in winter
There is a section devoted especially to edible flowers and leaves which
are particularly useful in salads.

Suffolk Herbs
Sawyers Farm
Little Little Comard
Sudbury
Suffolk
Tel 0789 227247

Open for viewing on Saturdays only
Will send seeds by post but plants are available from the nursery

Wells and Winter
Mere House
Nr Maidstone
Kent
Tel 0622 812491

Open daily from 10.00 a.m. to 5.00 p.m.
Plants only available

Index

lentil and walnut salad 112–13
lettuce 33
lime dressing 177

magret de canard 153
mangetout peas 33
  and beanshoot vinaigrette 77
  and mint vinaigrette 122
mango 33
marjoram 20
mayonnaise, various 177–9
Meaux potato salad 94
Mediterranean
  chicken salad 156
  pepper salad 65
melon 34
  and grape salad 125–6
  and prawn vinaigrette 62
Middle Eastern salad 10
mint 20–1
minted melon and grape salad 125–6
moutarde de Meaux 14
mozzarella and tomato salad 145
mung bean salad 110–11
mushrooms 35
  courgette and red pepper salad 105
  marinated 105–6
mustard 14
  dressing 179

nasturtium 21, 23
  salad 87–8
nuts 35
  as garnish 15

oils 12–13
okra 35
  salad 118
olive oil 12
onion 35
  and orange salad 120–1
  with yogurt and coriander 121
orange
  and apricot salad 170–1
  and beanshoot salad 77–8
  dressing 177
  and onion salad 120–1
oriental
  chicken salad 155
  tofu salad 147

palm hearts 35
  and paw paw vinaigrette 60
pan bagna 139
papaya, see paw paw
parsley 21
parsnip 36
  with curry vinaigrette 116–17
pasta
  with courgettes and tomato 102–3
  pesto 102

and shellfish salad 161
  salad 141
paw paw 36
  and palm hearts vinaigrette 60
pear 36
  and Roquefort salad 82
pepperonata 66
  peppers 36
  and aubergine salad 65
Persian rice salad 99–100
pesto vinaigrette 185
pickled radish salad 123
pineapple and strawberry salad 166–7
pinto bean and courgette salad 110
pot marigold 23
potato 37
  and bacon salad 136–7
  celery and ham salad 95
  and mustard salad 94
  niçoise 136
  and prawn salad 135
  salad 138
  salad, curried 93–4
  salad, hot 93
  and tomato salad 94–5
prawn
  and avocado salad 58
  and melon vinaigrette 62
  and potato salad 135
primrose 23
pulses 30
purslane 21

radicchio 37
  and curly endive salad 83
  and Roquefort salad 83
radish 37
  and arame salad 113
  as garnish 16–17
  pickled radish salad 123
  and sesame vinaigrette 122–3
rainbow bean salad 109
raspberry
  and blackcurrant sundae 165–6
  vinaigrette 176
ratatouille 69
red cabbage and walnut salad 80
red kidney bean and rice salad 134
rice salad 99–101, 134, 160–1
rocket 21
Roquefort
  dressing 184
  and pear salad 82
  and radicchio salad 83
rose petals 23

safflower oil 13
salad sandwich 139
salade
  cauchoise 95
  de chèvre grillée 64–5